The Black Goddess Collective Presents:

The Path to Pleasure

DEDICATION

◆ ◆ ◆

To all the Black women pouring from an empty cup: Take a break. It's time to heal.

You deserve to live every day of your life full of joy and ease. As a Black woman, you deserve to heal the wounds of suffering, striving, and let go of the burden of strength (you know, the "be strong for everyone else" narrative).

Now is the time to shift from overworked and overwhelmed to satisfied and inspired. Let's unlock your deepest desires. Because, in this sacred space, we believe all things are possible.

The Black Goddess Path to Pleasure book is an invitation to step into your feminine power, begin to release old traumas, and tap into your deepest desires, which may be buried or forgotten.

"A woman who begins to heal herself, heals her daughter, her mother, and heals every woman around her."

- Anonymous

TABLE OF CONTENTS

SETTING THE STAGE/CONTEXT/WHY THIS TOPIC, WHY NOW?

◆ ◆ ◆

Are you a professional Black woman who feels overworked, underappreciated, and just plain old exhausted? Have you lost touch with the feminine side of yourself? Or maybe you feel blah about life.

Between navigating life, work, and family, things can feel fast-paced, demanding, and stressful. It's easy to get lost in the sauce and end up at the bottom of a long, ever-growing to-do list.

Black women are groomed to carry heavy weight, to suck it up, to endure—all while still getting shit done.

Throughout your life, you may have experienced trauma that impacts your femininity, including physical abuse, sexual abuse, pregnancy, menopause, fibroids, breast cancer, weight gain or loss, or shame and guilt surrounding the topic of sex.

Did you know that these traumas can often be stored in the womb space? Have you acknowledged the impact that these traumas may have had on you sexually, mentally, emotionally, and spiritually in order to begin to heal and transform?

It's time to ask what happened to YOU.

YOUR pleasure?

YOUR satisfaction?

YOUR heart's desires?

But life's constant grind, putting the needs of partners, children, family, and friends ahead of our own, didn't allow you to do deep healing work.

It's time to rest your superwoman cape, sis.

The biggest drug is suffering. Decide not to tolerate stress, frustration, anxiety, depression, overwhelm, and shift to happy, abundant, playful, and grateful.

You're in the right space because this book offers an in-depth exploration of practices to help you honor your body, heal from trauma, awaken your life-force energy, and connect with the core of your divine womanhood.

Are you ready to come home to your inner goddess?

Do you want to open up your pleasure potential and fully embody your feminine power?

Would you like to enjoy more vitality, more energy, and a more fulfilling sex life?

Then turn the page to meet your guides: Tosh Patterson and Regine Monestime.

Oh, wait, but real quick. Ladies, this content ain't for the faint of heart. If you're a prude, unwilling to speak about or willing to explore often taboo subjects (sex, masturbation, yoni, etc.), this one ain't for you.

Our Path to Pleasure book content is for you if...

-You'd like to explore how sexuality opens the path to pleasure in all areas of life

-You'd like to feel more alive, inspired, and juicy daily

-You'd love to experience more pleasure and orgasmic juju

-You're curious to discover parts of yourself you haven't met yet

-You're open to having a deeper connection with the innate wisdom of your body

-You're ready to awaken to your deepest desires and begin creating a new lifestyle journey that's dripping with pleasure

-You're willing to explore taboo topics around womanhood

-You're ready to examine blocks and obstacles that prevent you from letting go both spiritually and sexually

WHAT YOU'LL LEARN

◆ ◆ ◆

As Black women, we must understand the importance of the relationship between sex and the soul. We are three-part BEINGS with mind, body, and spirit, so we must honor and connect with the Divinity of each layer.

Although there are many ways to reconnect with your true self, we believe that pleasure is an untapped and underutilized way to heal what is going on in your life. We could have written a book about meditation, etc., but what's missing is something for us, as Black women, on a subject matter we rarely discuss in our upbringing and education. Sexuality and pleasure are aspects of ourselves that, if we make peace with and can begin to heal, can bring so much peace. It's a part of our nature we ignore.

Too many of us have wounds from sexual abuse and past hurts that need to be healed. Plus, who doesn't want better, more fulfilling sex? Science even tells us that people who have sex more are happier and healthier than those who don't. And if we can have the knowledge and learn tools to bring peace to that part of ourselves, we can experience many of the desires we truly want—the life we desire. Finally, the more empowered women are in the area of their sexuality, the more empowered they will be in other areas as well. When women can learn to unabashedly ask for want they want in the bedroom, that courage will help them ask for what they want in the boardroom as well.

After reading this book, you'll walk away with new knowledge and have the tools and rituals to apply to your life. Specifically, you'll learn:

1. The Black Goddess Code. Living by these principles will allow you to awaken, heal, transform, and access your deepest desires.

2. Sacred healing practices to guide you on the path to pleasure. Each practice can become a ritual in your life to nurture your Goddess energy. You'll find tons of simple things that will make a huge impact.

3. That sexuality can be sacred and holy and can be seamlessly integrated spirituality.

4. Basic framework of the chakra energy system and how to use it for healing and growth.

5. How to receive more bliss and pleasure in all areas of your life, despite life's challenges.

Now, if you're ready to reclaim your birthright of sexual pleasure and power, turn the page.

DISCLAIMER

◆ ◆ ◆

*We are not medical professionals. In good faith, and with pure intentions, we are sharing our lived experiences and knowledge to support Black women in creating a life they love.

MEET TOSH AND REGINE

◆ ◆ ◆

When two intentional Black women meet, it doesn't take long to connect deeply. Especially when both are willing to be vulnerable and share their passions. That's what happened when we first met in 2018.

And in a short, yet miraculous time span, we've bonded in ways that take some a lifetime, and now we help each other in a spiritual-conscious relationship and support each other's dreams. We believe in the power of sisterhood, healing and sharing, and it was from these values that this project was born.

But before we came together, we were on our own path, experiencing life, learning lessons, and getting our asses kicked from time to time.

We quickly learned that we had a shared narrative, all too familiar for the Black woman's story—one of shallow success, struggle, and heartbreak.

As we compared notes, it became clear that we both had a lived experience of sheroism, ("I got this" "I can do it myself"), followed by defeat (smack down), and an eventual return to our true selves.

Before we share the lessons that inspired the Black Goddess Path to Pleasure, we would like to share our personal stories.

TOSH'S STORY

◆ ◆ ◆

Honey, my yoni has been through some things. Despite being a recovering perfectionist, I can say out loud that I'm coming to you with battle scars from being stressed out and overextended. Today, I live a tuned-in, turned-on life, which means I'm led by my internal GPS, and am living a life I love that's filled with peace of mind and less stress, but it wasn't always this way.

Abuse

We live in a world where abuse, both domestic and sexual, is an unfortunate reality. In fact, 45% of women have experienced sexual abuse. I'm one of those women. I grew up surrounded by domestic violence.

When I was young, both my grandmother and mother were in violently abusive relationships. Luckily, each found the courage and strength to leave, but being in that environment during my developmental years had a negative impact on feeling safe and secure in the world.

At the age of 13, my trust in others was further damaged as a victim of sexual abuse. In hindsight, I can see that experience resulted in becoming unconsciously disconnected from my body.

In college, I went to therapy to begin healing. Before going to graduate school, I decided to tell my parents about the abuse. Telling my truth was such a relief since I'd been carrying that secret for years. They called a family meeting to check on the other kids and confirmed no one else had been abused. Then, just one day later, with my family in the room, I confronted my abuser. It was a scary but liberating moment.

Sis, if you are a survivor of domestic or sexual abuse, I stand with you in solidarity. You are more than your past, and your mind and spirit are capable of healing. This, I know for sure.

The most embarrassing story

Fast forward to my adult years, and I had successfully followed society's success script: go to college, earn advanced degrees, secure a good job, climb the corporate ladder, get married, buy a house.

All checked!

There I stood in this thing called life, with my superwoman cape blowing in the wind, feeling proud to have checked off each box of society's script.

In 2010, my days were fast-paced. At that time, my to-do list was never-ending. I'd earned two promotions at work, so I was part of the executive management team. Each moment of the day was packed—starting before work by reading emails over breakfast, followed by going from appointment to appointment with barely a moment to escape for lunch, never mind restroom breaks.

On this particular day, I darted into the restroom to change my tampon and realized it wasn't there.

No string.

No tampon.

Nothing. The whole thing…just MIA.

There I stood, confused as to how it could be MIA when I knew, without a shadow of a doubt, I had inserted a tampon.

I was HORRIFIED!!!! Why me?

I couldn't recall any of my friends EVER mentioning losing a tampon. In a panic, I went to YouTube to learn if others had experienced it. No luck.

Then I proceeded to call my best friend. She, too, hadn't heard of it.

My mom said something similar happened to her many years ago. "Go to the gynecologist," she said.

So, one day later, there I was on the exam table, talking to my gynecologist.

Doc: It's not there. In fact, there's nothing there.

Me: Are you sure?

Doc: Positive. Nothing there. Maybe it slipped out.

Me: But I would have felt that. Are you sure it's not lost inside me?

Doc: I don't know what else to tell you, but I'm certain it's not there. Did you even put one in?

Me: Silence.

There I was, all propped up on the table, thinking, *Did I put a tampon in?* I had been so busy, rushing from place to place, going from thing to thing, I couldn't even remember if I had used a tampon.

Geesh, how could I be that disconnected from my body? At first, I felt crazy, then I thought, I CANNOT be the only one who is so busy, so rushed, so automated, that I do things without awareness. And I thought, *What kind of woman is that disconnected from her vagina?*

Hopefully, you haven't had a moment like this, but I'd be willing to wager that you're constantly on the go. You take care of everyone else, but what about your own self-care? Are you so overworked, overwhelmed, and inundated, you find yourself on the bottom of the list? Where is the time to connect with yourself?

Yoni Eggs. What?

Through the chaos of my embarrassing tampon moment, I realized I wasn't prioritizing the importance of my own self-care. I failed at allowing myself to believe it was possible. The entire thing was a sobering moment that caused me to be more concerned about how I could shift from frantic to calm, both personally and professionally.

After that experience, I understood the importance of carving out time for myself daily and began allowing myself to unplug and create some breathing room in my life. I freed up some mental space that was once reserved for stress and worry. Allowing time for rest resulted in me being more present, more ali\   re productive, and I want that for you, too, so we'll get into the how-to in the coming chapters.

Following the tampon incident, I wanted to be more aware of, and better in touch with my yoni delving deeper into my femininity. As they say, when the student is ready, the teacher arrives. A friend invited me to check out a yoni egg class. I had never heard of yoni eggs but attended the class, ready to learn and tap into my femininity. The yoni egg teacher opened me up to the world of yoni eggs, chakra healing, and many more things we'll discuss throughout the book.

My teacher and mentor helped me give myself permission to experience sexual pleasure, regardless of size. For a couple of years, I maintained a consistent yoni egg practice. I began practicing Bikram Yoga, learned about chakras, mudras, and connected to my feminine glow. During those years, I tapped into my feminine energy and unapologetically made time for self-care.

Career Burnout/The Crash

Then, out of nowhere, the pace of life seemed to be getting faster and more frenetic, thanks largely to advances in technology, which meant more email, social media pings, and on and on. My work life and personal life were often rushed and mashed together in a blur of activity. The high-speed pace, hustle, and constant grind started to pull me down. I rarely took any days off and even began banking 'use or lose' vacation time. I started feeling MEH.

My self-care diminished, and I stopped using yoni eggs.

The fast-paced lifestyle crept back in and that, coupled with stress and overwhelm, resulted in me feeling shell-shocked, disconnected, and disinterested in my career. I could see that for more than 15 years, I had worked to check off every item on society's success list, but I still felt empty, wondering if THIS was all there was in life and with work?

When I graduated with a master's degree, I was ready to take over the world, but after 15 years of doing what I had studied and had been trained to do, I hit a slump. I didn't love it anymore. All the magic was gone. My career felt like a steamy summer romance that went from hot and heavy to fizzled in what seemed like an instant.

Yeah. My career, my life…it felt like that: FLAT.

So, day in and day out, I pushed myself to keep up with emails, daily tasks, attending meetings, and supervising staff, but neglected to prioritize myself as I had previously. Then, eventually, it caught up with me.

There was a period, maybe 18 months, where I would drive into work and sit in the parking lot, bawling my eyes out. I'd have a good cry, dry my tears, and walk to my office. It was a difficult time when I felt stuck and wasn't sure how to get out of the corporate matrix. My boss micromanaged, and as a Black woman, I did not feel valued, seen, or heard. I was so sick of working at such a demanding pace, but I couldn't leave yet because I needed the money. Plus, from the outside, it seemed like I had it made, so people, including my husband, didn't truly understand my complaints/burnout/perspective.

All the stress from career demands compounded in my body and resulted not only in massive weight gain (hello, stress eating) but also unhappiness. Having such a push-push-push mentality drove my spirit into the ground. I was grumpy most days, and during those years, I hated my life because I was jumping through hoops and going through the motions to get my biweekly paycheck, but in my heart of hearts, I knew it was time to leave.

That level of unhappiness and uncertainty triggered stress. I began experiencing excessive bleeding triggered by stress. I had irregular periods and heavy clotting (think chunks of blood, like Jell-O, discharging from my yoni), but all tests came back fine. Of course, things were not fine. After an extensive battery of tests, and several consultations with my GYN, I decided to have vaginal surgery to scrape my uterus lining. The entire ordeal created worry. I did not feel sexy nor did I want to have sex.

I slid into a major funk that ultimately resulted in me hitting rock bottom physically (gained 90lbs), mentally (gave up hope for leaving my job), and emotionally (withdrew from life).

My Path to Pleasure/Healing

These hardships with my yoni and life pushed me into a deep dive with my soul. I took one day at a time, and after a TON of self-help books and classes, I started unlocking MY success script, not society's. I finally accessed my own feminine intuition and began to access my true, authentic self.

During my deepest, darkest valley, I found that teachings from Louise Hay, Michael Bernard Beckwith, and Wayne Dyer helped shift my mindset. For more than a year, I immersed myself in daily wellness practices like meditation, Bikram yoga, sound healing, and essential oils. And, not to sound cliché, I began to heal my mind, body, and spirit.

Simple, joyful pleasures on my healing path included:

- returning to yoni egg practice
- yoni steams
- fresh flowers weekly
- traveling to retreats
- detoxing from social media
- not watching TV or any news
- working with energy healers
- meditation
- massage
- soothing baths with Epsom salts
- decluttering my space
- reconnecting with my husband, emotionally and sexually
- self-pleasure/exploring my body
- restoring the balance of my 1st and 2nd chakra with guidance of an energy healer

Exit Strategy/The Plan

These are the self-care routines that pulled me out of that bleak place. As I climbed out of my valley, I created my personal exit strategy, reviewed and discussed it with my husband, and began putting the plan into action.

Over 6 months, I executed the plan. With the support and partnership of my husband, I:

- **Sold our single-family home.** Initially, this was hard for me because I was attached to my big, beautifully renovated house, but my husband kept pushing me to consider selling our house because he could see the negative impact of staying at a straining job. I EVENTUALLY began to see the house was out of alignment with the type of life I wanted to live, and my ego, not me, wanted to keep the house. Throughout the process, I had to remind myself, "I am perfect, whole, and complete," with or without the house.
- **Took a $20k decrease in salary.** Ouch. I wasn't ready for such a big financial hit, but I left my soul-sucking, dream title job because I wanted peace of mind more than anything else. I FINALLY left a toxic work environment and transitioned to another position, all with the focus of eventually launching my business.
- **Paid off $15k joint debt.** Despite my salary decrease, together, we paid off more debt than ever before. We got clear on what we each really, really wanted to have, then purged or sold the rest. The decluttering of physical stuff energetically opened up space to receive true desires. At the time of writing this, we have $5k remaining in debt and have set a goal to pay it off in a couple months.

All of these pressure points unlocked a new life—one now designed by my inner GPS system. Today, I'm a perfectly imperfect work in progress. I am a woman of power, healing myself, awakening my authentic desires, and unlocking my bliss.

A big, BIG part of my story, and what I like to share with other women, is my experience of career burnout and stress. As high achieving women, it's all too easy to define ourselves by career and material status. The ego clings to superficial things.

Society, familial, or cultural definitions of success may work for a while, however, eventually, Y-O-U have to be satisfied with your life, and it becomes burdensome to your spirit to live your life according to another's standards. If you're holding on to something because you feel like you *should*, or *have to*, I invite you to give yourself permission to have what you want.

So, as I said at the start, my yoni and I have been through some things from sacred, embarrassed, ashamed, and overwhelmed to successful, vibrant, and triumphant.

Taking time to create quiet, sacred space for myself has been, and continues to be, important in my own healing pathway. I had to truly acknowledge my own traumas and get clear on my deepest desires in order to begin balancing my mind, body, and spirit.

There's a universal principle that like attracts like and, as the universe would have it, when I took action on my exit strategy, other women, such as yourself, showed up, wanting help to shift out of overwhelm and stress in order to tap into more freedom, more time, more money, more joy, more peace of mind.

You're in the right place, my dear! If healing and abundance are available for me, it's also available for you. Regine and I are eager to share how you, too, can get to the other side.

REGINE'S STORY

◆ ◆ ◆

As a reformed attorney and Strong Black Woman, my life was filled with uphill battles, proving myself, and doing it solo. I was that chick. Living by the mottos: "It's better to look good than to feel good," "I got this," and "I'm good, I don't need no man to…"

But what that got me was shallow success, serial dating, and feeling empty inside. But I hid it well and looked good doing it. Sharp, savvy, sassy, and aloof, I was quick to humor, proficient at avoiding going deeper, and because I was so smart, I outsmarted others (or at least I thought) into not digging too deep.

The price I paid for that I had always had a feeling of low-level anxiety. Feeling like things could be taken away from me at any moment, which always left me feeling a little off-balance.

At one of the highlights of my career, as the legal advisor to public officials and administrators, I was making great money, and I was the shit. Let me insert here that I didn't like most of the people I worked for. I wasn't crazy about politics at all, but I had to play the game to keep my gig. Appearance was everything.

My somethin' tol kept telling me to leave, and I knew I should, so I told her, "Yes, I will, I just need a little more time."

Well, time ran out, and before I could gracefully make my exit on my terms, I was fired.

Yup. There was an actual coop. People were after me. WTF! Me? I'm nice. The polite, friendly lawyer. Why are people after me? I didn't do anything to anyone.

Those lessons my mom told me started replaying in my head. "It was too good to be true. You can't trust people. Don't make waves. Get a good job and stay there no matter what." I knew inside I didn't want to stay, but I was too afraid to do what I really wanted. Eventually, that which I feared the most came to pass.

And when that day came, it was so humiliating. Can you imagine sitting on stage, televised, being told that you were fired? "Y'all couldn't come to me ahead of time and ask me to politely resign? It had to be in front of the world?" I didn't deserve this. Why, God? Don't I pray, go to church sometimes, and am basically a good human being? I had no idea at the time that life was calling me for something else. I just thought I was being victimized, punished, and hated on.

Now what? This wasn't on my personal agenda. It wasn't supposed to go down like that. What was I going to tell future employers? That I was fired? That scenario didn't exist in my image files.

I was so embarrassed and felt like the worst thing that could have happened to me had happened. After crying for over a week, I decided to do what everyone does: look for another job. I re-worked my resume so being fired didn't look as bad as it was, highlighted my skills, put on the dog and pony show, and got back out there.

I felt like Jerry getting beat up by Tom in the cartoon. Every time I didn't get a call back or didn't make it to the next interview, it was a punch in the face, stomach, and head. What was wrong with me? Why couldn't I find something? I felt like I had no choice. I had to keep going, so I hired two different resume writers and a career coach. I went to networking events, career fairs, called colleagues from law school, old jobs—any and everybody who could help.

Now, I was the villain WWF wrestler getting booed by the crowd and getting my ass kicked all over the ring. Body slams and head butts, it was brutal. Nothing was happening for weeks and months. An interview here and there, but every time I saw something that looked promising—body slam.

Several months later, my ego was pretty much decimated. I couldn't make another call, send my resume to one more place, or go to one more interview. It was too humiliating.

So, I decided to take a break.

I needed to get away—run away. Leaving was what I really wanted to do the entire time. Go somewhere new, where no one knew me, and start over. I had always admired those people who sold everything, moved to a new place, and figured it out, but I was way too conservative and too focused on following the success road map to allow for that big a risk.

Instead, I opted for the next best thing in my mind, something a little safer: traveling. I visited family and connected with people who loved me no matter what. I retreated.

I went to a retreat center alone and spent time in reflection and contemplation. I sat by a lake and rested, attended group meditations, and prayed. Thankfully, I had a library full of self-help and spiritual books and went through years of training, courses and study, so I studied.

I had nothing but time to connect with God and really understand what eluded me. The more questions I asked about why this was happening, the more I heard, "Be still and know."

The more I sat in silence, the more my soul settled. Eventually, a break, a heart opening, glimmers of light. I was reminded that all things work together for my good.

I started to open myself up to the possibilities of what I really wanted and instead create a career and livelihood I loved. I started to take baby steps in the direction of my dreams. And with each step, I gained a little more clarity and more confidence. For years, I knew that I loved to travel and wanted to somehow create a business that involved travel. I also loved all things spirituality, personal growth, and development. If there was a book that had the word "path," "guide," or "journey" in the title, I was all over it. I studied personal development and spirituality for years. I was a retreat junkie who loved going on retreats to disconnect.

What if it was possible? I decided to take a few more steps and invest in a coaching program to learn more about travel and retreats.

And when my coach told me that I could actually create a career doing what I loved and make good money. "Really? Naw, who would pay me to lead them in retreats? I don't have a pastoral degree, I'm not a psychotherapist; what can I offer?"

And she said, "Are you kidding, Regine? You're amazing. You have so much to offer women. You have to learn how to step into your calling. You can do it, love." The tears rolled, but I didn't believe it for myself.

Why didn't I believe it? I knew I was smart, but why wasn't I more confident? I'd been studying spirituality for years, so why couldn't I manifest and create the life I wanted? What was I doing wrong? During my time retreating, I realized that I had a lot of information but didn't really have knowledge and wisdom. It was all in my head, but not in my heart. So, with the help of my coach, the stack of books about spirituality, self-development, success principles, science and metaphysics that I had read and re-read, and lots of prayer and meditation, I took the scary journey from my head to my heart.

During that process, I was able to consolidate long-standing, proven spiritual practices that I put myself through repeatedly to make sure they could be replicated with consistent results. It helped me gain the confidence, clarity, and compassion (especially for myself) I needed to be happier as well as have the courage I needed to follow my dreams. I was able to grow closer to the God within me, and know without a doubt, who and what I am.

My business, Black Butterfly Journeys, was born. I created a business out of my interests, skills, and passion, rather than society's expectations, and because my cup was so full, I knew I needed to pour into others.

After my metamorphosis, I became a butterfly and realized there are so many other women like me who aren't living their best lives, but who knew there's more to life than what they see. Some women have been hurt, experienced loss, and know that having a closer relationship and being one with the Divine is a missing piece in their lives.

Knowing that made me realize that other women were also struggling with their purpose and passion.

At some point, it hit me that maybe I had gone through a career fail to bring me through what was necessary to start a business I love, that helps bring other women through as well.

What if getting fired was the best thing that ever happened to me?

Now, my life is about consistent spiritual practice, attending regular retreats, and getting the support I need. Life is more amazing than I'd ever imagined. I am truly happy, full, and grateful.

WHAT IS THE BLACK GODDESS PATH TO PLEASURE?

◆ ◆ ◆

The Black Goddess Path to Pleasure begins with an intention to guide you in awakening your pathways to greater sexual pleasure and spiritual connection. We believe the integration of sexuality and spirituality is a sacred, loving, and honoring practice and way of life.

As facilitators of The Black Goddess Path to Pleasure, we create sacred space for Black women to come together, join in sisterhood, and honor our body temples. We come together to release what no longer serves us, free our inner wild, wise woman, and reclaim the Divine Feminine within.

The purpose of this book is to support you in:

-Understanding the relationship between sexual pleasure and spiritual connection. We will learn paths to connect to spirit, profound healing and pleasure through our deepest essence, our sexual energy.

-Having the best, most meaningful sex of your life NOW, with or without a partner.

-Experiencing pleasure as a path to healing (explore the Healing Power of Pleasure).

-Experiencing a sexual shame breakthrough! We reclaim our birthright to our authentic power, deep love, and acceptance of ourselves.

-Cultivating greater self-love, energy, and happiness! We will begin to explore Divine Feminine sexual healing, and you will experience the power of feminine healing.

-Providing tools/rituals you can apply to your life.

...because healing comes from accessing your life force. And life force is sourced by sexuality.

...because it's time to SAY YES TO PLEASURE and make that a standard for life.

TRANSFORM

◆ ◆ ◆

Again, we intend to help you understand the connection between sexual and spiritual bliss.

If you're live in the room with us, or reading this book, you'll feel restored and renewed knowing exactly how to access your feminine power.

Plus, you'll re-connect to your Divine Feminine nature and be unapologetically committed to experiencing pleasure in all areas of your life — your one and only RIGHT NOW life.

As a creative being, you can own and step into your feminine powers and claim your desires. You have the ability to tap into and direct your yoni energy to manifest untapped dreams and restore balance in all of the affairs of your life.

Honey, are you ready to be tuned into your Spirit and more turned on by your life?

Imagine: more joy, more pleasure, more creativity, and even more juicy orgasms ☺

It's time to heal your yoni and claim your Black Goddess energy.

HOW TO USE THIS BOOK

◆ ◆ ◆

Self-care is a divine responsibility because acts of self-care uplift and replenish your soul.

Doing small things for yourself every day is necessary to keep your cup full, overflowing, and satisfied. In a nutshell, you cannot perform your life's purpose if you do not put yourself first. This is about putting on your own oxygen mask before helping others when the plane goes down.

In the back of this book, you'll find sacred, healing practices to guide you on the path to pleasure. Each practice can become a ritual in your life to nurture your Goddess energy. You'll find tons of easy, simple things that will make a big difference. Give yourself permission to take what you want and leave the rest. This book is not meant to overwhelm you or make you feel like you aren't doing enough. Instead, we hope to give you tools and resources to leverage life daily. Making the time for at least one of them every day will make a huge difference. Taking the time to do at least ONE of the things on this list daily will keep you from hitting physical, mental, and emotional exhaustion. This type of self- care will shift you into a state of receptivity and teach you how to nurture yourself.

BLACK GODDESS CODE

These are regular actions/rituals you can commit to in order to nurture your goddess energy.

- Weekly 30-minute bath soak
- Weekly self-pleasure
- 15 minutes of daily joy
- Enjoying naps
- Drink water daily
- Asking for what you really, really want (not just what you think you can get)
- Daily body movement
- Weekly time in nature
- Engage in one healing practice or ritual daily (see resources at the back of the book)

"Use sexual energy to heal yourself and establish an intimate connection with yourself and partners."

LESSON 1:
Yoni Anatomy

◆ ◆ ◆

There's a tremendous amount of confusion, fear, distortion, and wounding around the topic of sex in Western culture. Women, Black women, in particular, have been diminished by popular culture and marketing advertisements telling us what "sexy" means.

Since being transported to America, certain archetypes have plagued how we, as Black women, are seen by society and, consequently, how we see ourselves. You know what we mean, right? The "workhorse, superwoman," "aunt Jemima maid," "the abstinent, good, Christian woman," "the oversexualized Jezebel," "angry Black woman," "the welfare queen," and on and on.

Each of these archetypes has done serious damage to our self-esteem and don't portray us as healthy, whole, sexual beings.

And when you add the staggering sexual abuse statistics to the mix, we understand why we've naturally been fearful of sex and intimacy.

Many of us have run to the church for guidance and support without recognizing that religious dogma can often lead to the suppression of our natural sexual nature.

For example, many women turn to complete abstinence out of guilt and fear of judgement. Their painful pasts and unhealed wounds cause them to reject the possibility of intimacy and connection with others, and even themselves.

Much of these behaviors get passed down consciously and unconsciously from generation to generation.

We are taught:

Sex is dangerous.

Sex will get us in trouble.

Sex is shameful.

Sex is not spiritual.

Good, Christian women don't enjoy sex.

As a result, we have a screwed-up relationship with sexuality. Sexuality is sometimes so repressed, a mother may not have the thought, knowledge, or vocabulary to teach her daughter about her own body or vagina. So, of course, there's no exploration of the sacredness of the vagina, and we forfeit deep pleasure that is available to us because we're disconnected from our bodies.

These unconsciously inherited beliefs are so pervasive in the Black community, they seem normal. And many of us don't realize how much they affect us. How do you know if something is wrong? Nod your head if you can relate to any of these:

1) You don't regularly experience blissful, full-body orgasms.
2) You ignore what you want as unimportant, or don't ask for what you want sexually because you're afraid, don't know how, or think it's not important.
3) You have difficulty letting go sexually or having immensely pleasurable sex with yourself and others.
4) You believe that masturbation is wrong, a sin or immoral.
5) You seek or have sought out sexual experiences that are risky and potentially harmful because you want to be liked, loved, or want to be in a relationship.
6) You avoid, don't enjoy, or believe that women shouldn't want or desire to initiate sex.
7) You've decided sex isn't important and haven't had sex with yourself or others in over six months.
8) You're embarrassed or ashamed of your body, so you cover it up, don't look at it, and criticize yourself.
9) You don't like to be touched, hugged, and avoid human contact at all costs.

10) You've been a victim of sexual abuse and haven't healed from it.

11) You overcompensate and over give to your own detriment. You'll set yourself on fire to warm others.

12) You people please and allow yourself to be mistreated.

13) You allow others to take advantage of you by not providing or doing their part while you do the heavy lifting at work or home.

14) You're not knowledgeable about your vagina and womb.

15) You don't believe there's a relationship between sexuality and spirituality.

Is it just us, or can you see we have issues with sexuality?

MEANING OF YONI

◆ ◆ ◆

W e want to introduce you to your anatomy. Your God-given, sacred lady parts.

In our teachings, we use the word yoni to refer to and explain the vagina. 'Yoni' is the Sanskrit word for the female genitals, meaning 'sacred space' or 'temple'. In ancient traditions, our yonis were honored and worshipped for their life-giving abilities. However, in our culture today, we have lost this sense of honor and reverence for this amazing part of our bodies. We have chosen to use yoni in preference to vagina as it offers us the opportunity to reclaim the sacredness and power of our sexuality as women.

In many spiritual teachings, the yoni is where the Shakti lives, which is the universal creative energy.

What that means is our womb and yoni is a place to access our wisdom, our power, our creativity, and our life source. Think about the fact that we all come from this extraordinary, magical, profound place. We invite you to reconnect with yourself, honor yourself, love yourself, and celebrate yourself as a spiritual, sexual being.

Do you know that the clitoris' only purpose is pleasure? Other body parts have multiple purposes, but not the clitoris. With 8,000 nerve endings, its sole purpose is for your pleasure.

Your yoni is its own beautiful and vibrant ecosystem. It's time to learn and understand your womb space. Once you have the vocabulary for your yoni-verse, you can better direct a partner or explore yourself. The lack of knowledge and understanding creates lack of pleasure and/or trauma because we don't understand our bodies.

Now, for an anatomy review:

- **MONS VENERIS**: fatty tissue mound over the pubic bone
- **LABIA MAJORA (big)**: outer lips rich with pubic hair. This area is sensitive to touch but not as sensitive as labia minora or other parts of the clitoris.
- **LABIA MINORA (small)**: inner lips. Sometimes protrude out of outer lips. Surround clitoris head and entrance into vagina. Extremely sensitive and play an important role with arousal. Highly sensitive area.
- **CLITORAL HOOD**: fold of skin that protects clitoris. Comes in all shapes, colors, and sizes. Powerful source of pleasure.
- **CLITORAL HEAD**: protected by hood of inner lips. The clitoral head has 8,000 nerve endings, more than any other part of the body. Often called the love button.
- **INTROITUS**: leads to vaginal canal.
- **VESTIBULE**: outer vulva area.

YOUR PLEASURE ANATOMY

❖ ❖ ❖

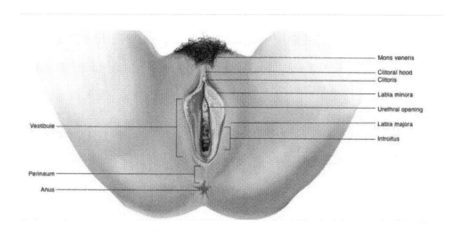

Your body is an amazing, glorious gift. In addition to your beautifully designed yoni, she has a few other amazing features:

1. **Your yoni is a self-cleaning microcosm.** Despite what we may have been raised to believe, there's nothing dirty about your yoni. Using products internally changes the PH balance of your vagina, which can be harmful.

2. **Your yoni protects itself from items getting lost in it.** Nothing can get lost in your yoni, so it is not some infinite, mysterious space. The internal area is a finite space, and whatever you place inside yourself will come out with a bit of wiggling and shaking.

3. **Your yoni will tell you if something is wrong.** If there's abnormal discharge, itching, burning, discomfort, pain, or irritation, your yoni is telling you something is out of balance.

4. **Your yoni is capable of immense pleasure.** We don't mean the old run-of-the-mill, sneeze-like clit-gasms, but also the kind of pleasure that feels like you're melting into the universe. Why? Because you have a clitoris with 8,000 nerve endings, and there are also lots of nerve endings inside the vaginal canal that allow for maximum pleasure. The clitoris isn't the only source of orgasm, and there are multiple types of orgasmic states women can experience if willing to devote time and energy to exploration. And, remember, your amazing clitoris' only purpose is to give you pleasure. Yup! That's its only function. No other body part can claim that distinction.

5. **Your yoni can birth another human being.** You already know this, but it's amazing that your yoni has the capacity to give birth. There can be soreness and tearing, but generally, afterward, things return to normal and functional over time. Magical. Mind-blowing.

Now, you have the proper vocabulary and description of each part of your pleasure anatomy!

Get a mirror and take a picture of the anatomy to get to know yourself. What does your clitoral hood look like? What shape are your inner labia? This simple practice is something many women have never done, so it can be quite an empowering experience of discovery!

In closing, we invite you to explore and reconnect with your yoni. We invite you to send her love and healing thoughts and to begin to spend quality time with her.

"Your spiritual journey has nothing to do with being nice. It is about being real, authentic. Having boundaries. Honoring your space first, then others."

LESSON 2:
Acknowledging Trauma

◆ ◆ ◆

So many of us don't know about our bodies and yonis because we've endured so much trauma over the years and that trauma has disconnected us from our yonis and bodies. Instead of feeling comfortable touching and exploring ourselves, we totally shut off and are not knowledgeable about our own anatomy.

That's why we want to start with you reconnecting with your beautiful body, to get to know her again or for the first time. And now, let's talk about what this T-word is all about and how we can finally face and move past these wounds and hurts.

Do you know what's blocking your pleasure? Are you aware of old hurts you have been carrying that negatively impact your feminine energy?

It's time to uncover the blocks. Let's begin to focus on uncovering hidden trauma.

Some traumas are obvious, like physical or sexual abuse, disease, and medical conditions. Others are more subtle, like shame, guilt, stress, and fear. All are damaging, painful, and can stop us from experiencing pleasure, connecting with ourselves and others, and puts our bodies in a constant state of moving between balance and imbalance.

As you read this, can you identify past traumas that you believe may have prevented you from experiencing a joyful, fulfilling sex life? If you aren't familiar with your yoni, or feel uncomfortable touching and exploring yourself, are you able to pinpoint what could have happened to contribute to your disconnected relationship with yourself?

If you haven't been able to point to all of the events that have happened to you that may be classified as trauma, take a look at the list below to see if any of these examples look familiar.

Here are several examples of trauma:
a. **Physical abuse.**
b. **Sexual abuse/rape.**
c. **Pregnancy.** While giving birth can be beautiful, some women have not had positive experiences and, as a result, become disconnected from their yoni.
d. **Unwanted changes to the body.** Changes such as scars, hysterectomy, weight gain or loss, and aging can negatively impact body image.
e. **Diseases.** Such as breast cancer and fibroids—unfortunately, fibroids are a Black woman's issue.
f. **Masculine imbalance aka Strong Black Woman Syndrome.** Black women often operate in dominant energy, which creates an imbalance and, over time, limits range of emotions/way of being.
g. **Lineage.** Much of our trauma gets passed down from our parents and caretakers. For example, our limiting beliefs, fears, and insecurities were probably taught to us from an early age.
h. **Racial trauma.** This can be a book in and of itself. The untold damage of racial trauma shows up in our lives and impacts how we see ourselves, what's possible for us individually, and as a race.
i. **Shame and guilt.** These are more subtle forms of traumas and look like your inability to look at yourself lovingly and to touch yourself pleasurably. You may not feel comfortable in your skin and hide from yourself or others.

How did you do? Did you identify any as being part of your experience?

The truth is, if you live long enough, you'll experience some trauma. And what happens to many of us, whether we acknowledge it or not, is that these traumas get stored in our bodies, in our yonis, and create discomfort, stress, dis-ease, and disconnection from our sexual pleasure and creative powers.

Part of healing comes from acknowledging the traumas and healing the wounds so you can feel whole and complete, fully love and accept yourself, receive joy and pleasure in all its magnificent forms, and create a life that's based on your wildest and most expansive dreams.

Unfortunately, most of us are not able to honor, heal, and forgive traumas, so we struggle and fight through life. But it doesn't have to be that way. As energetic beings, we are governed by an energy system that, if open and balanced, will allow energy to freely flow through us and even help propel us to live happy, healthy lives.

Chakra Energy System

This energy system is comprised of seven main energy centers containing bundles of nerves and corresponds to major organs as well as our psychological, emotional, and spiritual states of being. These energy centers are called chakras in Sanskrit, which means "wheel of light" and in the Yogic teaching represents separate levels of consciousness.

When each chakra is open and working together, they enable us to lead by our open heart, freely communicate our desires, and use our creative energies to manifest them.

Imagine you're a pipe drain. If you allow too much hair or gunk in the drain, water can't flow freely. If your drain is in a bathtub, then the bathtub will back up with water, stop, and eventually, bacteria and mold will grow. Yuck! The same is true for our bodies and chakras. If we're clogged up energetically, and have too much drama and stress in our lives, it will be impossible to allow the abundance of the Universe to flow into your life naturally and easily.

The reverse is also true. If your chakras are too open, then you end up taking on other people's stuff, end up over-giving and miss out on your blessing.

So what does this have to do with your traumas? Well, because much of our trauma is stored energy, you can't cure them with a pill and can't always reason them with your mind. Rebalancing your energy centers or chakras are a proven and effective way to heal old, hardened traumas that are sometimes even older than you.

Let's explore the chakra system and learn how to rebalance them to create more health and flow in our lives.

Overview of Chakra Energy System

The first three chakras, starting at the base of the spine, are chakras of matter. They are more physical in nature.

1st Root Chakra/ Color: Red

o   The chakra of stability, security, and basic needs. It encompasses the first three vertebrae, the bladder, and the colon. When this chakra is open, we feel safe and fearless.

o   It represents our foundation, our feeling of being grounded, and it is related to our contact with Earth Mother. It is also the centre of manifesting things in the material world.

o   Emotional issues: Survival issues such as financial independence, money, and food.

o   Physical issues: Problems like obesity, anorexia nervosa, and knee troubles can occur. Root body parts include the hips, legs, lower back, and sexual organs.

2nd Sacral Chakra/ Color: Orange

o   This chakra is our creativity and sexual center. It is located above the pubic bone, below the navel, and is responsible for our creative expression.

o   It represents our connection and ability to accept others and new experiences. It holds the basic needs for sexuality, creativity, intuition, and self-worth. It is also about emotions and friendliness, and is the seat of our creativity, confidence, and sense of self-worth.

o   Emotional issues: Sense of abundance, well-being, pleasure, sexuality.

o   Physical issues: Kidney weakness, stiff lower back, constipation, and muscle spasms. Belly body parts include sexual organs (women), kidneys, bladder, and large intestine

3rd Solar Plexus Chakra/ Color: Yellow

o   The third chakra is our source of personal power. It covers the area from the navel to the breastbone. It represents our ability to be confident and in-control of our lives. It is our centre of personal power, the place of ego, of passions, impulses, anger, and strength.

○ Emotional issues: Self-worth, self-confidence, self-esteem.
○ Physical issues: Digestive difficulties, liver problems, diabetes, nervous exhaustion, and food allergies. The body parts for this chakra include the stomach, liver, gall bladder, pancreas, and small intestine.

Connection Between Matter and Spirit

The first three chakras are related to our physical world, the higher chakras are related to our spiritual world, and the heart is the bridge between the two.

The fourth chakra serves as the connection between matter and spirit. Located at the heart center, the fourth chakra is in the middle of the seven and unites the lower chakras of matter and the upper chakras of spirit. The fourth is also spiritual but serves as a bridge between our body, mind, emotions, and spirit. The heart chakra is our source of love and connection. When we work through our physical chakras, or the first three, we can open the spiritual chakras more fully.

4th Heart Chakra/ Color: Green

○ It is our centre for love, compassion, and spirituality. It affects our ability to not only love others, but to love ourselves as well. It also connects the body and mind with spirit.
○ Emotional issues: Love, joy, inner peace.
○ Physical issues: Heart attack, high blood pressure, insomnia, and difficulty breathing. Body parts for the fourth chakra include the heart, lungs, circulatory system, shoulders, and upper back.

5th Throat Chakra/ Color: Blue

○ The fifth chakra is our source of verbal expression and the ability to speak our highest truth and is located in the area of the throat. The fifth chakra includes the neck, thyroid, and parathyroid glands, jaw, mouth, and tongue.
○ It represents our ability to communicate and is the centre of sound and expression of creativity via thought, speech, and writing. It is also the location for the possibility of change, transformation, and healing.
○ Emotional issues: Communication, self-expression of feelings, the truth.

O   Physical issues: Hyperthyroid, skin irritations, ear infections, sore throat, inflammation, and back pain. Body parts for the fifth chakra are throat, neck, teeth, ears, and thyroid gland.

6th Third Eye Chakra/ Color: Indigo

O   The sixth chakra is also referred to as the "third eye" chakra - center of intuition and is located in between the eyebrows. We all have a sense of intuition, but we may not listen to it or heed its warnings. Focusing on opening the sixth chakra will help you hone this ability.
O   It represents our ability to focus on, and see the big picture. It is also the centre for psychic ability and higher intuition.
O   Emotional issues: Intuition, imagination, wisdom, ability to think and make decisions.
O   Physical issues: Headaches, blurred vision, blindness, and eyestrain. Body parts for this chakra include the eyes, face, brain, lymphatic, and endocrine system.

7th Crown Chakra/ Color: Violet

O   The seventh chakra is the chakra of enlightenment and spiritual connection to our higher selves, others, and ultimately, to the divine. It's located at the crown of the head. It represents our ability to be fully connected spiritually.
O   Emotional issues: Inner and outer beauty, our connection to spirituality, pure bliss.
O   Physical issues: Migraine headaches and depression.

Because we each have different traumas and experience trauma differently, we may each need to focus on rebalancing different chakras connected to our wounds.

For example, you may have trouble speaking up for yourself or asking for what you want. That affects your sixth chakra, located at your throat. Or you may not be able to connect with people in a real and authentic way. That's a heart chakra issue. As you understand your traumas more, you can learn to diagnose your particular wound and use tools through the chakra system to begin to heal yourself.

If you're here because you resonate with traumas related to sexuality, then we invite you to really explore your first and second chakras as they represent your relationship to your foundation and sexuality, which, for many of us, is the beginning of it all.

In closing, we hope you now understand that trauma can impact your chakra system, as well as your femininity. Having at least a basic knowledge of the chakras can significantly deepen your healing process and journey inward. You have the power and ability to tap into your chakra energy to restore yourself.

"I am going to live the way I want to live. I am going to live in my own spontaneity and authenticity. I am not here to fulfill anybody's expectations."

[Oxum(Oshun) the Goddess of fertility and beauty]

LESSON 3:
Black Goddess Healing Tools

♦ ♦ ♦

In this chapter, we're going to share specific ways of how you can align your chakra energy system and intentionally begin repairing chakras that may have become too open, too closed, congested, blocked, or damaged. Using and practicing the Black Goddess Healing Tools will strengthen your relationship with your yoni and sexuality.

Awaken your inner goddess with these sacred practices for healing, self-love, and embodying the Divine Feminine essence within.

These are tools that have worked for us and have proven to be effective, and you'll learn why. One of the reasons we've been talking about the energy centers and chakras is because energy work is so important to healing, but for so many of us, it's a new or foreign concept. We typically try to resolve our issues through talk therapy or medicine. There's nothing wrong with that, but a big piece that's missing for many of us is energy work.

We said that trauma is sometimes invisible—you can't always touch it or reason it away—so we need tools that go beyond the physical dimension.

Are you ready to awaken, heal, and balance your chakra energy system?

Black Goddess Healing Tools

Black Goddess Healing Tool #1 Chakra Meditation & Visualization

HEALING TOOL: Chakra Meditation & Visualization

WHAT IT IS AND WHY IT WORKS:

Meditation is the best way to maintain the optimal function of your spiritual energy.

When you're in a meditative state, you're connected to your body, mind, and spirit. The truth is, we have the power to heal our bodies, and practicing meditation allows your body to do what it naturally wants to do, and that is to repair itself.

Used in connection with the chakra system, meditation can improve the balance of your key chakras and bring your health and mental attitude into a more peaceful state.

Because your chakras are part of an intimately connected system, and one chakra impacts another, it's a good idea to meditate on all of them to bring the entire system into balance. With time and experience, you'll get better at detecting individual imbalances and directing your meditation to focus on particular chakras that are out of sync.

To get started, find a peaceful and quiet place where you won't be disturbed for at least fifteen minutes.

Sit comfortably on the floor with your legs folded in front of you, or on a cushion or chair. Hold your spine erect, but not stressed. Relax your body. Breathe deeply and evenly.

Take each chakra in turn, from the root to the crown. As you do, you should picture the energy flowing into and through that chakra. You can use the color associations of each chakra provided above during your meditation.

Start at the root chakra, move up to the sacral chakra, then the solar plexus chakra, heart chakra, throat chakra, the third eye chakra, and finally, the crown chakra, infusing each with the life-giving energy.

Give each chakra attention and focus on it until you can see vibrant energy passing through it or you feel it's time to move on to the next one. Each chakra deserves several minutes for itself, and you'll use the power of your imagination and visualization as you move through each chakra.

Move up to the crown chakra and see the energy leave the top of your head. The last step in chakra meditation is to visualize all the chakras at once, being fed by this energy coming in from the breath and up from the earth. See the chakras and your aura become brighter, clearer, and supercharged from this life-giving energy.

Finally, open your eyes and relax a couple minutes. Pay attention to your body and how incredible and energized you now feel. If you're just getting started, it might be helpful to use guided meditation to help you focus on the different chakras and the associated color.

PERSONAL EXPERIENCE:

Regine

For years, my meditated practice was on and off, hot and cold. If something was wrong, I would go in, and if everything was fine, then I'd stop. As a result, my life was constantly in rollercoaster mode. It wasn't until a few years ago that I really started to take my spiritual practice seriously and decided that no matter what, it comes first. And when I did that, everything changed. I began to go into deep states and then began to explore other tools, like visualization and chakra healing. And when I did that, I made big shifts. My life changed rapidly. I feel amazing, have a business I love, relationships that work, and things come much easier for me now. I know for sure that I wouldn't be where I am today without these powerful tools.

Black Goddess Healing Tool #2 Self-Pleasure Practice

HEALING TOOL: Self-Pleasure Practice

You may be thinking, why on earth would I want to have a self-pleasure practice?

We know. We totally get it. It's not something most people talk about over dinner—it is hardly spoken about at all! It's a subject that can hold a lot of charge, and it's a practice that most people want to keep private.

But the reality is, having a Self-Pleasure ritual is an essential practice for all women, whether single, dating, or in a relationship.

Why? Because Self-Pleasure is a practice.

A practice in loving yourself no matter what.

A practice in connecting with yourself before you connect with the world.

A practice in filling your own cup first so that when you do go out into the world, you are overflowing.

A practice that gets you connected with everything.

A practice where you have to drop everything and be present with what is—in the moment and in your body.

Really, it's just like meditation!!

During orgasm, the awareness of the identity or ego is dissolved,, so in that moment, you are dis-identified, and you can touch your infinite nature. This is why sex and orgasm have have been used as a tool in spirituality to reach higher states of consciousness. Orgasm has been called the 'mini death' because it erases a sense of separate self. Your sexual practice can be used as a doorway to achieve enlightenment, in fact.

Plus, benefits of Self-Pleasure:

- To fall deeper in love with yourself
- To help you feel sexier and more connected to your body
- Prioritize your own needs, rather than always putting others first
- Get really good at receiving
- Begin to increase PLEASURE in all areas of your life

WHAT IT IS AND WHY IT WORKS:

We live in a world where most women are totally disconnected from their pelvic area, from their physical yoni, and their innate feminine wisdom.

We have chronic tension in this area. We don't like the way our vagina looks, or we have sexual trauma from being penetrated too many times when we weren't totally ready, or when we didn't invite the experience.

We don't KNOW this part of us.

We don't talk about it.

We don't take the time to truly discover it and make FRIENDS with our beautiful yonis.

But there are so many ways to do this, starting with self-pleasure.

Self-Pleasure can serve as a spiritual practice because you can deliberately use this sexual energy in a conscious way. Here are two primary reasons this practice works:

(1) Self-pleasure enhances self-intimacy, and subsequently, other-intimacy. Developing intimacy with yourself is critical if you want to be intimate with someone else. To be intimate with yourself, you need to see yourself, feel yourself, hear yourself, and understand yourself. When you master this, you have a sense of self to bring into relationships with others. And you'll be better able to offer intimacy to someone else. It is important that you are familiar with yourself sexually, and self-pleasure is one of the best ways to develop this self-awareness and self-familiarity. You'd be surprised how much you can learn about yourself by just engaging with yourself in a sexual way. As we've previously stated, some women have avoided thinking about, touching, or educating themselves about any part of themselves that they consider sexual, which alienates them to such a degree, they avoid intimacy and sex. If you are disconnected from your

body, you cannot direct sexual intimacy with another in a way that would be pleasurable to you. What that means is, you're at the mercy of your partner, who has no idea what you like and don't like, want and don't want, because you don't either. This can make your sex life, and even your relationship, troublesome. To avoid yourself sexually is a state of resisting yourself. This is not healthy, and fuels shame.

(2) When we feel pleasure, we come into a state of emotional, mental, and physical alignment, and it brings us squarely into the present moment instead of maintaining a state of resistance where we are lost in the past or the future. This level of awareness opens the chakras and energy channels, and we have much more life-force energy flowing into and through our being. When we are out of alignment, illness begins to manifest. So, by bringing ourselves into alignment, we amplify the healing process and add to our overall health. The body responds to that alignment by following suit. For example, it releases oxytocin and endorphins, which relieve pain. The immune system is mobilized, and blood flow increases throughout the body, which further nourishes our body. Our cells begin to have better respiration, and the portion of our brain that is associated with fear and anxiety goes dormant. The bottom line is, self-pleasure can help keep us physically healthy.

HOW TO:

Enjoy your **Black Goddess Self-Pleasure Practice.** Before each session, gather things you will need:

(1) Set a date in your calendar for a weekly self-honoring practice. This time is to be non-negotiable, just like a meeting or yoga class, as it is such an important part of self-healing.

(2) A timer so you won't be distracted by looking at the clock and thinking about the time. If you use your phone timer, put your phone in airplane mode to not disturb your practice.

(3) A space to indulge. Select a space that you can relax and feel safe.

(4) A notebook to journal about your experience.

(5) Any toys or sensation implements that may serve your intention for exploration. You can use crystals, yoni eggs, or other toys. Remember, this practice is not about having an orgasm alone. Instead, we invite you to explore using toys or trying positions you may not usually try.

(6) Place your hands over your heart and set an intention before every session. Example: "My intention is to explore my body and be present to the sensations I am experiencing" or "I melt into the feminine energy and receive the abundant pleasures that fill my life."

(7) Melt in your Exploration. Healing. Pleasure. Rub your body. Moan. Massage your breasts. Touch your head. Admire your thighs. Say to yourself, "body beautiful."

(8) Savor your practice. A key aspect of this practice is savoring. Take time to feel your body after the practice; to deeply feel the sensations you've created—pleasure, relaxation, arousal, etc. Use the last five to ten minutes of your practice (or one minute if you're doing a five-minute practice) to lay, sit, or stand in stillness, breathing deep and savoring what you've created in your body (similar to savasana in a yoga class).

EXERCISES/ PRACTICES:

1. Touch your vagina regularly - make her part of your life.

2. Use a hand mirror to look at your yoni and notice what arises.

3. Talk to your yoni and develop a relationship of trust - cultivate a sense of awe of her power and wisdom.

4. Use a wand or tool (like cervical serpent) to gently massage the inside (with preparation) to release points of tension and contraction.

5. Yoni Massage Therapy is a powerful modality that can support you in healing the pelvic area, releasing tension and creating space, but also EMOTIONALLY and MENTALLY through cultivating a healthy relationship with our pelvic space and ourselves as women.

6. Intimate touch - Hold partner's genitals. If you're not having sex with a partner but wish to stay connected, simply touch each other by cupping. Often, when we are busy, we can feel disconnected from our sex centre as our head becomes the main driver. This is a great way to support your partner to stay embodied and connected to themselves deeply. It also helps break down a preconceived belief that when genitals are being touched, it means SEX is next. This belief is what stops a lot of people from starting any kind of intimacy with their partner because they feel that if they start, they are obligated to do more. Once this belief is broken down, and the pressure or expectations connected to it disappear, a whole wide world of fresh and new ways to be intimate opens. Make sure to do this at different times to get the complete benefit of this. Hold your partner's genitals and look into each other's eyes. It's also OK to close your eyes to drop into your body sensations, both as giver and receiver, but I invite you to try it with your eyes open at some point as it will increase your intimacy. Breathe deeply and notice how you feel. As the receiver, really relax and allow yourself to be held and let your body open.

PERSONAL EXPERIENCE:

TOSH - YONI MASSAGE

I first discovered the magic that is Yoni (vagina) Massage when I began studying yoni eggs in 2015. I attended a retreat, and the leader (another married Black woman) explained Tantric Massage with Yoni Massage and encouraged attendees to feel the effect of this unique style of bodywork.

My whole body melted. I was in total ecstasy, feeling all kinds of incredible sensations I'd never felt before.

I was experiencing my body in a completely new way—*THIS* is my body!?

At the same time, the sensations went beyond the body, somehow. It felt like I was expanding into the universe and simultaneously dissolving into nothing.

I was profoundly peaceful. It was a deeply sensual experience, but not exactly sexual, even though she gave me a Yoni (vagina) Massage as part of the session.

My yoni felt incredible. More alive than ever before, yet deeply connected to the rest of me—my sexuality blending with my whole being rather than being focused on the genitals.

Sensations that originated in my vagina became part of a background buzz of immensely relaxed pleasure.

Eventually, the massage was over. I knew it was 2 hours long, but time ceased to have any meaning for me during the experience. I walked out on a cloud, my body tingling from head to toe, feeling gloriously alive and awakened.

My mind was well and truly blown.

I was high for days afterward (in a good way!). I was also surprised. In awe. A bit confused. How come no one had told me about this?

Of course, every experience was different—sometimes, it was also challenging, confronting, emotional, or healing. Usually, it wasn't a sense of sexual pleasure, but more so beautiful feelings in that area—deeper sensitivity, more connection, more awareness. A relaxation and a softening. More love for this part of the body.

I knew I'd come across something special, and I wanted to share it with as many women as I could, so I did!

Black Goddess Healing Tool #3 Yoni eggs

HEALING TOOL: Yoni Eggs

Yoni egg practice was initially used by ancient Taoists to cultivate feminine sexual energy. Ancient practice surfaced in ancient China, and for a long time, it was kept a secret practice that was only available for members in the royal family. Yoni Eggs are also known as the secret Feminine weapon. The eggs are semiprecious stone (from natural earth) carved into an egg shape and polished to be worn inside the vagina. The stone egg practice has been used for strengthening, sexual and spiritual fortification, tightening, and energetically cleansing the vagina for over 6,000 years.

Sacred Nourishment for Women

Muscles are trained through resistance and the use of weights. Regular Kegels will only minimally (or not at all) strengthen your pelvic floor and tighten your vagina. When you utilize a yoni egg and practice Kegel exercises, you're entering a whole new realm of power. With yoni eggs, you are essentially engaging in vaginal strength training, ensuring your muscles work harder and grow stronger, creating a subtle, strong, and nourished vagina.

The pressure from the yoni eggs works with the muscles inside your vagina through a series of contractions and releases. With yoni eggs, your vaginal muscles have to work to keep the egg inside by closing and constricting around it, lifting and releasing it without the egg falling out. Depending on size, yoni eggs are slightly weighted to add the perfect amount of resistance.

Yoni Eggs are like your very own personal trainer for your lady bits!

You might find that after a few short weeks of doing daily exercises, you notice dramatic changes in your vagina, regardless of your age. Exercising the yoni is just as important to your well-being as working out at the gym and eating a healthy diet, and it's safe to say that the benefits are limitless.

By beginning this journey, you're increasing the sensitivity of your vagina, creating more vitality and a more vibrant/alive environment within your most sacred space. Within a week, yoni egg exercises can enhance the sexual pleasure and potency of any woman (and man) lucky enough to know about them.

WHAT IT IS AND WHY IT WORKS:

By placing the egg in the vaginal canal, it causes the stone to rest on the pelvic floor muscles, and the added weight tones the vagina, along with:

- Awakening the tissues and muscles that will promote new nerve growth
- Increasing Increasing overall sensitivity
- Increasing libido
- Increasing natural lubrication even after menopause
- Balancing estrogen levels
- Gaining control over your vaginal muscles and rocking your lover's world
- Reducing PMS, menstrual cramps and duration of your menses
- Improving well-being
- Massaging the reflexology point in the vaginal wall
- Helping remove trauma from the womb
- Increasing blood flow and oxygen to the vagina
- Enhancing vaginal elasticity
- Enhancing sexual pleasure
- Recovering after childbirth
- Receiving the healing energy of each crystal

HOW TO:

Drilled vs. Undrilled Yoni Eggs

One of the most common questions we get asked is, what is the difference between the drilled and undrilled yoni eggs?

Most women prefer a drilled yoni egg because you can attach a string (dental floss, natural hemp, or something natural since it will be inside you) to have control of your yoni egg. Think of it like wearing a tampon; when you are ready to remove your yoni egg, you gently pull the string and out comes your yoni egg. You can also use a string to do exercises with your yoni egg.

How to insert:

Inserting your yoni egg is simple and fun. We recommend inserting with the tip pointing down, however, either way is perfectly fine. Inserting a yoni egg is just like inserting a tampon with no applicator.

Also, remember, your yoni egg can't get stuck! It can only go as far as your cervix, which acts as a wall, keeping her within the vaginal canal only.

How to Remove:

Removing your yoni/jade egg is simple. Get into a deep squat position and push out with your vaginal muscles. If needed, you may use your fingers to scoop the yoni egg out or jump up and down. If these techniques don't work, sit on the toilet, spread legs wide, and relax your muscles, which will help the egg fall out. For string users, give it a gentle tug (think removing a tampon) and allow her to glide out slowly and easily.

EXERCISES/PRACTICES:

How to Practice with Yoni Eggs?

Simple Kegel exercises are the foundation of the yoni egg practice. The great thing, though, is you can reap the benefits by simply wearing it! The egg is working its magic regardless. In fact, if you have never done Kegel exercises before, it is best to ease into the practice and start your routine by just wearing your yoni egg for the first two weeks. The egg will engage the muscles that would usually stay dormant and can result in some interesting new sensations and awareness.

How to use a Yoni Egg

Once your yoni egg is in, there are a few different ways to use her:

- Exercise
- Meditate
- Yoni breathing
- Sex (alone or with a partner)

Exercise vaginal muscles:
The most common use of the yoni egg or jade egg is strengthening vaginal muscles through Kegels. Simply insert your yoni egg and begin Kegel exercise.

Meditate:
Use the yoni crystal to meditate, hold her in your hands, inside your vagina, on top of your womb, or wherever you feel she is needed. Begin to relax, clear your mind, and connect with your spiritual self. Let the energies flow through your yoni egg and yourself.

Have sex with her:
This is best done with a smaller sized egg. Insert your yoni egg and get her into a comfortable position. Try nudging her up in the g-spot region. Play and enjoy the pleasure she brings. Be careful not to let the yoni egg hit your cervix with too much pressure to cause pain or bruising.

Yoni breathing:

The practice of connecting with your yoni and sexual energy. Insert your yoni egg into your vagina or hold your yoni egg on your womb. Begin to inhale and exhale with your mind and body focused on your yoni. As you inhale, squeeze your vaginal muscles, and as you exhale, release your vaginal muscles. Be sure to be in sync with your squeezes and breaths. Use this time to focus on you, your body, sexual energy, and bringing out your feminine side.

Yoni Exercises

Yoni eggs and jade eggs were designed to enhance Kegel exercises by adding weight and resistance. To begin using a yoni egg, insert her into your vagina with the larger end going in first. If you have a drilled yoni egg, the tip with the string will be pointing down. Once the jade egg is in place, you can begin using her!

Kegels:

The practice of contracting and releasing your pelvic floor muscles. Properly performed Kegels can be tricky. Make sure you are only contracting your pelvic muscles, not your butt, abs or thighs. Once you have identified the pelvic floor muscles, you're ready to start kegeling!

The perfect Kegel: Doing your Kegels correctly is vital when working with your yoni/jade egg. You first want to make sure you are contracting the correct muscles. To do so, contract your pelvic muscles without flexing your abdomen, thighs or buttocks. Your pelvic floor muscles are like a hammock that holds all your womb parts up and in place. If you are having a hard time finding your Kegel muscles, try laying on your back or try using the restroom and stopping your urine midstream. Make sure not to hold your breath, you should be able to breathe through your contractions.

- The basic: Start by contracting and hold for 5 seconds, then relax. Once you can hold for 5 seconds, try longer intervals of 10-15 seconds. Repeat contractions for 5 minutes a session.

- The quickie: Contract and hold for 1 second, then relax. Continue the 1-second intervals for 5-minute sessions.

- Combine the basic and quickie for an advanced 5-10 minute workout.

Make sure to use your yoni egg or jade egg for the optimal workout!

Kegels can be performed standing up, sitting, or lying down.

If you are a beginner and your yoni egg won't stay in, try lying down on your back while you do your work out. Once you have trained and strengthened your muscles, try standing up during Kegel exercises.

PERSONAL EXPERIENCE:

Tosh

This story is embarrassing but funny.

Within the first 24 hours of using my yoni egg, I thought it was lost inside. I couldn't get it to come out, despite doing the squatting and pushing the teacher recommended. Nothing was working.

In a total panic, the morning of the last yoni egg class, I asked my husband to help me remove it, and after 15 minutes, the egg FINALLY came out. When I told my teacher, she laughed and said, "It can't get lost inside you."

Ah, yes. True story.

At that time, that's how little I knew about my yoni-verse. So, I'll spare you the frantic moment and remind you that your yoni egg will not get lost inside of you. If you're using a drilled egg with a string, you'll be able to remove the egg easily. If you're using an undrilled egg, as I was, then you may have to be patient and allow your yoni to release when she's ready.

Black Goddess Healing Tool #4 Movement

HEALING TOOL: Movement

WHAT IT IS

When was the last time you got down or busted a move?

Singing and dancing is a positive way to align your chakras! Your soul is happy when you are moving and using the power of song to send positive vibrations through your energy, body, and soul. When you are singing and dancing, you are turning your brain off, which qualifies as a meditative act. You lighten up, feel free, and learn to step outside of your comfort zone.

Movement brings you to the present moment.

Movement like belly dance, yoga, walking, and free flow dance connects you with your body.

Intentional movement, of any kind, can help awaken your sexual/sensual side because the music can be sensual, with rhythmic drum beats, conjuring up images of desserts, mystery, fire, and the exotic.

By moving your body in ways you may never have before, opening the pelvis, and rocking the hips, this releases your sexual energy (oo-err). Belly dance activates these areas to open them up and help you become more conscious of them.

Whether you believe in things like chakras (and how the pelvic sacral chakra is blocked if you have low desire) or not, moving the hips in this way creates a sense of sexual charge or energy that will help you begin to make your way back to feeling a sense of desire.

Lastly, adding music to movement creates another healing layer. Everything (including you) is about vibration and balance, therefore, sound and vibration play a fundamental role in your life by affecting physical, mental and spiritual. Sound healing allows you to: raise your energy, release yourself from stress, expand creativity and consciousness, and unlock your potential.

WHY IT WORKS: BELLY DANCE

(1) It's fun. You can have fun with belly dancing because you can laugh, sing, shake and bend your body however you feel. No one judges you, and there are women of all different shapes, sizes, and backgrounds who belly dance.

(2) It's not vigorous exercise. Instead of breaking a sweat, you'll be practicing how to wiggle your boobs up and down, shake your bottom and twirl your fingers like you're holding an invisible maraca.

(3) It's about enjoying yourself and the moment, and not about "performing" in any way. And having fun is a total antidote to stress, which is like a wrecking ball to the libido.

(4) It helps with body confidence. It looks so empowering b*ecause women of all shapes and sizes look sexy* and totally gorgeous while doing it!

(5) It creates a new relationship with your body. W*omen in the modern age often lack a sense of connection to their bodies.* We spend our days living in our heads, and the beauty of belly dance is that it forges a connection between your mind and body. Dance and using our bodies to communicate is one of the oldest forms of expression, and if we're disconnected from our bodies, and especially from our pelvic/hip region (*where, as women, our power resides*), it can leave us feeling deflated, empty, and lost. So, belly dance counters this through creation, expression, and teaching you to trust your body. If you stop "thinking" and let it move, it'll do so in ways you never imagined you could. It feels SO liberating.

(6) You begin to see yourself as a sexual being. Belly dancing helps you tap into the sexual energy you've misplaced. It's sensual, erotic, and feminine. The way you move your body, in some ways, imitates sex, so it gives you a language in which to express your sexuality.

WHY IT WORKS: YOGA

(1) Yoga is related to the chakra system because the asanas/positions help open those chakras. I.E.: hip openers are good for the second chakra, chest openers good for the heart.

(2) Each movement is about how to open and regulate the system.

(3) Movement allows energy to release from the body, consciously moving energy through our bodies.

(4) Also, it makes you feel good. Different rhythmic beats resonates with your root chakra, promotes healing and just makes you feel better.

HOW TO DO IT:

- Find a class.
- Begin an at-home practice.
- Watch videos.
- Dance to your favorite songs, alone, and do what feels good to you. Shut the door, draw the blinds, and do some serious dancing in your underwear! Next time a song comes on the radio, belt it out. Take your speakers into the bathroom and sing in the shower. Sing, dance, play; it is why we are alive.

PERSONAL EXPERIENCE:

Tosh

After many years of being ashamed of my body and feeling too big, I've built confidence by practicing yoga and belly dance. I like going to a physical class to practice and learn.

Yoga tunes me in to my physical body. I can feel muscles relaxing or joints calming with a stretch. However, belly dance drops me into a sensual, intuitive knowing. It's fun to shake my hips, shake my butt, and have fun with my body. When dancing, I don't worry, overthink or fear while moving and grooving. Afterward, I feel happier and lighter than when I began.

Regine

Daily walks are what keep me sane!

Walking is completely underrated! In my experience, a brisk walk is a perfect remedy to an anxious mind, a fatigued body, a hot temper, or depleted energy.

Depending on your intention, walking can serve many purposes. "Fast" walking or walking for an extended period of time will get your heart pumping and is considered cardio exercise. I can promise you my regular walks help keep my weight stable and my body in shape. A rise in heart rate activates the prefrontal lobe of the brain, which is responsible for emotional response. This boost in blood flow helps improve your mood dramatically.

Taking a stroll can also be turned into a walking meditation; however, if you intend to meditate, leave distractions (i.e., a dog) at home. While you walk, focus on the sound of your feet on the pavement. Be present and allow your thoughts to slowly leave your mind. Link your breath with your steps. Inhale, step, 1, 2, 3, 4. Exhale, step, 1, 2, 3, 4. It is best to take a walking meditation in your neighborhood or somewhere you feel safe. If you have to be on guard, your mind will not be allowed to turn off, and your energy cannot relax.

Finding 30 minutes of your day to devote to walking, moving, and breathing some fresh air can do wonders for your body, mind, and spirit. I recommend doing it at the same time every day so you can turn it into a habit.

Black Goddess Healing Tool #5 Forgiveness Practice

HEALING TOOL: Forgiveness

WHAT IT IS

To live is to get hurt. We've all been in situations where we feel others have done us wrong: by their words, their actions, or even worse, their indifference. And then there are the things we regret doing or saying ourselves. The saying is to forgive and forget, but in practice, we tend to hold on to our feelings of hurt and resentment.

Forgiveness is defined as a conscious, deliberate decision to let go of resentment or vengeance towards a person or group who has harmed you. Forgiveness is not forgetting or condoning or excusing offenses. It is what we do for ourselves to get well and move on. All of us have many things in the past we regret and would like to have done differently. In many cases, they are still with us in our thoughts, self-criticisms, and rationalizations about how this has prevented us from having the life we want.

Practicing forgiveness is a key way you can lead a more meaningful life and cultivate deeper happiness. However, forgiving someone—or yourself—isn't always easy. The act of forgiveness is a mind, body, and spirit ritual that will clear the decks of your mind and heart to create the space necessary for you to live with more love for yourself and others. This practice will help you achieve a deeper sense of peace and wellbeing. Once you know how to forgive, you eliminate excess emotional and mental weight that keeps you in repetitive situations, circumstances, and experiences that are not healthy or productive. By releasing the past, you have full energy of the present moment.

Forgive everyone, including yourself.

WHY IT WORKS

Forgiveness can soothe and heal you.

We understand the value of a bath to clean our bodies, and forgiveness acts like a bath for the mind. When we bathe our bodies, we wash away all the impurities from the day. Using soap and a towel, we cleanse our skin, sloughing thousands of dead skin cells. When we forgive, we wash away every mental and emotional impurity that holds us back.

Forgiveness really does have an inner power and renewing effect when we act with compassion and loving-kindness towards ourselves and others. It allows us to let go of many negative feelings and emotions that may be boiling like a pressure cooker inside of us, sometimes hidden and sometimes overtly felt. Forgiveness allows us to move on unblemished by our own wrongs or the wrongs of others. It is a gateway to peace, freedom, self-acceptance and greater ease in life.

If you are ready to stop feeling bad, stop being wounded, stop wondering why this or that happened, stop holding grudges, and stop giving yourself reasons and excuses to be, do, and have less than you desire, begin your forgiveness practice. Honestly, it may not be easy, but it is doable. So get yourself a beautiful Forgiveness Journal, a special pen, and begin.

HOW TO DO IT

PRACTICE 1 - 70x7

Step 1: Make a list of people you've held grudges against and wish to now forgive. Write their names in your Forgiveness Journal. Also, make sure your name is at the top of the list. Begin the process by forgiving yourself.

Step 2: In your Forgiveness Journal, write 70 times, I forgive _____. Do this for seven days for one specific person.

PRACTICE 2 - Forgiveness Meditation

If there are ways you have harmed yourself, or not loved yourself, or not lived up to your own expectations, this is the time to let go of unkindness toward yourself because of what you have done. You can include any inability to forgive others that you may have discovered on your part in the reflection immediately preceding—that is not a reason to be unkind to yourself.

During your meditation time, repeat this phrase: "For all of the ways I have hurt or harmed myself, knowingly or unknowingly, I offer forgiveness."

Continue this practice as a part of your daily meditation, and allow the force of intention to work in its own way, in its own time.

PRACTICE 3- Forgiveness Journal Prompts

To quote Edwene Gaines, author of *Prosperity*, who speaks about forgiveness as a spiritual law: "When we've carried a grudge (whether against ourselves or others) for many years, it can be hard to know how to start letting go. A good way to start is to write out exactly what it is you want to forgive. Seeing a statement of forgiveness clearly written out in black and white can be a powerful way to help you forgive when you haven't been able to before. Fill in the following blanks in your journal and see if that simple act doesn't help you start to release long-held grudges.

I am through feeling guilty about:_____

I am over feeling sorry for myself about: _____

I am finished with all sadness about:_____

I forgive my parents for: _____

I release all suffering about: _____

Above all, I forgive myself once and for all for: _____

It is done!

When you choose to forgive on a daily basis, you will find a lightheartedness begin to enter your life.

PERSONAL EXPERIENCE:

Tosh and Regine

We both used Iyanla Vanzant's book, *Forgiveness,* to go deep. It's a 21-day guide to forgive everyone for everything. Earlier, we shared our stories, so you can see the range of forgiveness work we needed to complete. If you want to focus on this practice, pick up Iyanla's book.

Black Goddess Healing Tool #6 Unapologetically Owning & Sharing Your Truth

HEALING TOOL: Unapologetically Owning & Sharing Your Truth

WHAT IT IS:

In African traditions, as well as most indigenous communities throughout the world, the village is everything. It is the place that feeds the community, provides safety, allows for connection and opportunities to experience joy, laughter, and fellowship. Many cultures use community as a gateway to spirituality and divinity, believing that where two or more are gathered, a powerful force—God—enters and dwells in that space.

In the West, however, we tend to rely on our individuality and use terms like "me" and "I" more than "we" and "us". The nuclear family is all that matters, and everyone looks out for themselves.

While there is certainly a place for individuality, and finding your unique place in the world, we lose so much when we rely on ourselves to provide everything we think we need, and focus on our individual needs versus the collective.

Americans are often isolated, lonely, and reluctant to ask for and receive help because our culture has us believing that you can and should do it alone and do it your way.

But the gift of community and the collective is a resource that is available to us if we use it.

WHY IT WORKS:

In medical and psychological therapies, group sharing provides healing for both the sharer and the listener.

When we realize that we're not alone, we feel less alienated and more empowered, which is a necessary ingredient to healing.

Having that "we're in this together" feeling and seeing others like you move through trauma, will help you know that you can do it, too.

Finally, being in a judgment-free and loving space heals the mind and soothes the soul.

HOW TO:

Think about and write down the top five things you'd NEVER want someone to know about you. Reflect on them and begin to own those as part of who you are. Consider how you can share that story/life experience from a place of power and have another person not feel alone or isolated as they hear about your hardships.

Now, write out all the things you're proud to have accomplished during your life. These triumphs can be much easier to share and are equally important to sharing/revealing the hardships.

EXERCISES/PRACTICES:

1. Find a support system, sisterhood, or retreat that resonates with you. Join us for a Black Goddess Collective Retreat where we do this work.
2. Make sure the space is safe, open, and non-judgmental.
3. Allow yourself to be fully present in the moment and engage fully in the experience. Be open, be honest, and share your story. It's up to you, of course, how often, when, and what you share, but remember that your sharing is part of your healing as well as the collective healing of the group.

Black Goddess Healing Tool #7 Yoni Prayers - Steps of Spiritualizing Sexuality

HEALING TOOL: Yoni Prayers

WHAT IT IS: Creating and manifesting your deepest desires by using sexual and spiritual energy

WHY IT WORKS:

Yoni prayers are another powerful tool that allows you to harness the power of your Goddess feminine energy to create your desires. Knowing how to accept pleasure in your life, from sexual pleasure to emotional and spiritual pleasure, will allow for more of it to show up for you.

Benefits of being more tuned into spirit and more turned on by life:
1. Learn/Create what you want
2. Have more pleasure and joy in general
3. Have better sex and sexual pleasure

HOW TO:

EXERCISES/PRACTICES:

Step 1: Awareness (knowing) of this fundamental truth that your yoni is the vehicle to creation. Divine Feminine as sacred space is source of creation in your life-Meditate, journal, and let it sink in.

Step 2: Acceptance- Open your legs and place a hand on your yoni and affirm, "I believe and accept that my Divine Feminine energy is sourced here. The path of creation". Meditate on that.

Step 3: Intention- Set your intention on creating/manifesting. Visualize something you want to create while keeping in mind your yoni energy. Imagine a powerful orgasm shooting from your root chakra like a fountain/rocket, propelling your desire into the atmosphere.

During partner sex, masturbation, or after orgasm, visualize what you want to manifest and let the sexual energy you have building up bring forth your desires.

Step 4: Gratitude- Give thanks in acknowledgment that it is done.

Step 5: Receive- Know that your prayers are always answered.

In summary, we've shared 7 healing tools you can implement into your life. When you practice these modalities together, it expedites your healing. We encourage you to pick one practice and be consistent with it. With all of these practices, we encourage you to take a deep breath and melt into this sacred time of self-love and pleasure. Earmark sacred self-care time for yourself every day for at least 15 minutes in order to implement the practice into your life.

Also, there are more practices under additional resources at the back of this book. We believe these are the seven primary practices to begin with, however, practices at the back of the book are also worthwhile, as long as you can establish a consistent practice for yourself. Be present with yourself enough to know what you need at any given point. There's always a solution—any of these can work.

Allow these practices to deepen your relationship with your sensual and sacred self.

CONCLUSION

◆ ◆ ◆

Black Goddess, congratulations on investing in yourself and taking this journey with us. We hope that you will step on the path to pleasure and find ways to nourish yourself, heal wounds, and nurture your relationship with all parts of yourself, including your yoni.

It is your divine right and responsibility to care for yourself, honor yourself, step into your power, and allow PLEASURE to fill every aspect of your life.

Be UNAPOLOGETIC ABOUT YOUR DIVINE FEMININITY.

HAVE CONFIDENCE to claim sacred space in a world that doesn't believe women should have power.

RECLAIM YOUR SEXUALITY for yourself, through your own body. Through your touch, your movement, your breath, your gaze. Your sexuality does not only exist in relation to others. It is part of YOU all the time.

Your sexual self is not something you need to harness or control, or force into submission. It is not wrong, bad, or shameful in any way, and it never could be. Not now and not ever.

We're talking about the very force that created us. It is inherently powerful, pure,, and sacred.

There is no point where you KNOW your sexual or sexual self completely; there's always more to discover. Layers of delicious exploration, always right there.

Isn't that beautiful?

We want you to use this book as a resource and keep it close by. We also invite you to plug into our Black Goddess Collective community to learn more about our other resources, retreats, and online/live workshops.

You can find us at: wetravel.com and search Black Goddess Collective

Because I am a Goddess, then…

_____
_____
_____
_____
_____
_____
_____
_____
_____
_____
_____
_____
_____
_____
_____
_____
_____
_____
_____
_____
_____
_____
_____
_____
_____
_____
_____
_____
_____
_____
_____

Dear Self, I love you and…

I create a state of heaven in my home by...

I choose to live my life on purpose, beginning with…

_____
_____
_____
_____
_____
_____
_____
_____
_____
_____
_____
_____
_____
_____
_____
_____
_____
_____
_____
_____
_____
_____
_____
_____
_____
_____
_____
_____
_____
_____
_____
_____

Today, I choose...

_____
_____
_____
_____
_____
_____
_____
_____
_____
_____
_____
_____
_____
_____
_____
_____
_____
_____
_____
_____
_____
_____
_____
_____
_____
_____
_____
_____
_____
_____

How can I make this current experience more pleasurable to myself?

_____

_____

_____

_____

_____

_____

_____

_____

_____

_____

_____

_____

_____

_____

_____

_____

_____

_____

_____

_____

_____

_____

_____

_____

_____

_____

_____

_____

_____

Write down everything you can appreciate in this moment...

Ask yourself what would make you happy right now. If you can, do it.

_____
_____
_____
_____
_____
_____
_____
_____
_____
_____
_____
_____
_____
_____
_____
_____
_____
_____
_____
_____
_____
_____
_____
_____
_____
_____
_____
_____

What can you do, now, to reclaim your body for yourself?

_____
_____
_____
_____
_____
_____
_____
_____
_____
_____
_____
_____
_____
_____
_____
_____
_____
_____
_____
_____
_____
_____
_____
_____
_____
_____
_____
_____
_____

What kind of woman do you want to show up as in the world?

_____
_____
_____
_____
_____
_____
_____
_____
_____
_____
_____
_____
_____
_____
_____
_____
_____
_____
_____
_____
_____
_____
_____
_____
_____
_____
_____
_____
_____
_____
_____

Where in your life do you need to slow down? Savor? Listen to your body?

How can you begin to feel more at home in your body?

_____
_____
_____
_____
_____
_____
_____
_____
_____
_____
_____
_____
_____
_____
_____
_____
_____
_____
_____
_____
_____
_____
_____
_____
_____
_____
_____
_____
_____
_____

List 3 things you can say YES to and 3 things you can say NO to.

_____
_____
_____
_____
_____
_____
_____
_____
_____
_____
_____
_____
_____
_____
_____
_____
_____
_____
_____
_____
_____
_____
_____
_____
_____
_____
_____
_____
_____
_____
_____
_____
_____

Describe your ideal session of long, delicious foreplay…

_____
_____
_____
_____
_____
_____
_____
_____
_____
_____
_____
_____
_____
_____
_____
_____
_____
_____
_____
_____
_____
_____
_____
_____
_____
_____
_____
_____
_____
_____
_____

Dear thighs, how I love thee. Let me count the ways...

(i.e.: You've carried me everywhere I've gone in my life. You are strong and powerful)

How do you stand in your beauty?

Goddess, you are fertile ground where anything you dream, desire, or even fear can grow. What seeds are you planting?

_____
_____
_____
_____
_____
_____
_____
_____
_____
_____
_____
_____
_____
_____
_____
_____
_____
_____
_____
_____
_____
_____
_____
_____
_____
_____
_____
_____
_____
_____
_____

Your sexuality and creativity are INTIMATELY linked. Fully embracing your sexuality allows you to fully express yourself creatively. List 3 ways you can accept more of your sexual self.

_____
_____
_____
_____
_____
_____
_____
_____
_____
_____
_____
_____
_____
_____
_____
_____
_____
_____
_____
_____
_____
_____
_____
_____
_____
_____
_____
_____

Are you sitting on your Goddess power?

_____
_____
_____
_____
_____
_____
_____
_____
_____
_____
_____
_____
_____
_____
_____
_____
_____
_____
_____
_____
_____
_____
_____
_____
_____
_____
_____
_____
_____
_____

The road to Liberation is paved in Truth. Your Truth. The whole truth. Be naked. Be honest.

Speak your truth about who you are, how you feel, your past, and your own lies.

_____
_____
_____
_____
_____
_____
_____
_____
_____
_____
_____
_____
_____
_____
_____
_____
_____
_____
_____
_____
_____
_____
_____
_____
_____
_____
_____
_____
_____
_____
_____

Does your self-pleasure practice feel holy and sacred? Can you fully receive pleasure?

_____

_____

_____

_____

_____

_____

_____

_____

_____

_____

_____

_____

_____

_____

_____

_____

_____

_____

_____

_____

_____

_____

_____

_____

_____

_____

_____

_____

_____

_____

Create your Pleasure List. Write down at least 5 things that are pleasing to you. How long has it been since you've enjoyed it?

_____
_____
_____
_____
_____
_____
_____
_____
_____
_____
_____
_____
_____
_____
_____
_____
_____
_____
_____
_____
_____
_____
_____
_____
_____
_____
_____
_____
_____

Seasons change. What can you do differently?

_____
_____
_____
_____
_____
_____
_____
_____
_____
_____
_____
_____
_____
_____
_____
_____
_____
_____
_____
_____
_____
_____
_____
_____
_____
_____
_____
_____
_____
_____

What is possible when you learn to love the skin you're in?

_____
_____
_____
_____
_____
_____
_____
_____
_____
_____
_____
_____
_____
_____
_____
_____
_____
_____
_____
_____
_____
_____
_____
_____
_____
_____
_____
_____

What is possible when you unravel the old dialogue about your body, gender, and sexuality?

What is possible when you embrace your full capacity for pleasure?

_____
_____
_____
_____
_____
_____
_____
_____
_____
_____
_____
_____
_____
_____
_____
_____
_____
_____
_____
_____
_____
_____
_____
_____
_____
_____
_____
_____
_____
_____
_____

What is possible when you embrace ALL of you and your sexuality?

_____
_____
_____
_____
_____
_____
_____
_____
_____
_____
_____
_____
_____
_____
_____
_____
_____
_____
_____
_____
_____
_____
_____
_____
_____
_____
_____
_____
_____
_____
_____
_____

You are your main source of power. Your pleasure consists of how turned on you are by your surroundings, your experiences, and yourself.

_____
_____
_____
_____
_____
_____
_____
_____
_____
_____
_____
_____
_____
_____
_____
_____
_____
_____
_____
_____
_____
_____
_____
_____
_____
_____
_____
_____
_____
_____
_____
_____

During a new moon, write intentions to bring the right people in your life or to call in what you wish to manifest.

"What if sexuality is religion AND self-pleasure is a personal prayer?"

ADDITIONAL RESOURCES & RITUALS TO IGNITE YOUR BLACK GODDESS ENERGY

◆ ◆ ◆

We provided 7 healing tools and suggest you begin with those. The rituals below can be coupled with the 7 healing tools to make your path to pleasure unique to your needs, likes, etc. Enjoy!

THE ART OF MAKING TIME FOR YOURSELF

10 minutes daily:

(1) Gratitude - honor/acknowledge 3 things

(2) Vision - imagine 3 things that if they happened 6 months from now, you'd be fulfilled

(3) Consider how you can love more TODAY and be more loving throughout your day

YONI STEAM

Womb Steams are an ancient practice that use the power of steam and the essential oils of dried herbs to cleanse, replenish, revitalize, relax, and restore the womb and vaginal canal, helping connect us with this most sacred center, releasing layers of stored trauma, both physical and energetic. During this ritual, we will each create our own herbal blend, mixing the herbs together in a large pot with steaming water and adding clear intention for what we want to heal and what we want to call in. Then, as we kneel over the steaming pot and allow the fragrant vapors to cleanse and nourish our bodies, delve deep into the healing process by engaging in the ancient practice of womb steaming and self-massage.

GODDESS BATHING

Life presents challenging moments. Everyone experiences at least low-grade depression, lack of energy, drive, or willpower. In these weak moments, draw a bath, make a sanctuary, steep your sorrow and sore muscles, and allow your cares to dissolve. Immersion in water is crucial for restoration. Create space for your healing and restoration by adding these elements:

Bath Soak:
-1 cup of Epsom Salts (like Dr. Teals Lavender) or use Himalayan Sea Salt
-3 drops of basil essential oil (or an oil of your choice)
-Splash of Apple Cider Vinegar (optional)

Optional:
-Candles
-Crystals
-Flower petals
-Music (no words)

Soak in bath for at least 20 minutes. When you stand and drain the bath, imagine all that no longer serves you, washing down the drain.

MOON RITUALS

At one time, human beings were more connected to earth elements. Due to technological advancements, we have lost the art of honoring the power of nature. Begin to reconnect with your Goddess energy by having a full moon or new moon ritual.

FULL MOON RITUAL

Full Moon Ritual is a time to release and receive. Google the date for an upcoming full moon. On the date of the full moon (regardless of it being morning or evening), write or speak these sentences:

-I release all sexual shame and fear that is keeping me from my erotic power
-I release any self-doubting thoughts that limit my sexual liberation journey
-I release sexual judgment of myself and of others
-I receive sexual autonomy, liberation, and abundance
-I receive daily moments of pleasure that connect me to my body and my desires
-I receive reclamation of my body, my desires, my love, and my erotic power

NEW MOON RITUAL

New Moon Ritual is a time to call in what you want.
-Create sacred space: light a candle, get flowers, crystals, pictures, oracle cards
-Cleanse self and environment: use incense/sage, take a ritual bath, tidy up
-Set intentions: plan, visualize, find your focus, dream, make a vision board
-Release and let go: visualize what doesn't serve you, write it down and destroy it (burn, tear up). Breathe deeply into your lower belly. Ask that the old energy/experience is released now. Exhale hard. Let go of the negative energy. Repeat often. Forgive/release

CONNECTION WITH DAILY AFFIRMATION CARD DECK

When I sit down with my decks each morning, it is like meeting an old friend. Each deck has a personality, different energy, and a unique gift of connecting me with other entities, spirit guides, and different realms. Through these cards, you form a relationship with your spirit guides and your own intuition.

Divine connection makes you feel secure and lowers anxiety because you learn to trust the unseen workings of the Universe, you discover your higher Self, you form a relationship with your Spirit Guides, and you don't feel alone anymore.

Draw one card, read the message, and open up to the possibilities/whatever thoughts or ideas come to your mind while you gaze at the image. Try not to analyze it too much. Get out of your left brain and trust your gut. What message is being sent? What comes to mind instantly? Do not dismiss any thoughts as imagination or coincidence. You have set the intention to connect, so whatever comes to you is divinely guided. Trust.

RELEASE RELATIONSHIPS

Before we came to earth, we signed contracts and made deals with other souls on how we would help one another in our human journey. Just as the earth goes through cycles of spring, summer, fall, and winter, we, too, have seasons, phases, and chapters of our big book of life. And most of the relationships in our lives are only intended to sustain a certain season; not all are meant to stay with us for a lifetime.

With the risk of sounding harsh, once a person, friend, or soul mate serves their purpose, it is time for us to then release the relationship. Clinging to any relationship that is no longer serving us can block both parties from continuing their soul growth.

When we release a relationship, it is never to be done in a spiteful or vindictive manner. Releasing another person is done with gratitude for their influence and help in your path.

Whether this person has brought you a happy memory or a harsh, traumatic event, their purpose had a powerful place in your life. Honor the relationship, never regret. Every connection we make in this life shapes us—it changes us and makes us who we are.

Write a letter to your friend, family member (yes, it is healthy to release family members), co-worker, etc. Tell them you are so appreciative of all the lessons they have taught you, thank them for all they have brought to you and the time you have spent together. Forgive them for anything that has happened in the past, and even apologize if you feel the need to get anything off your chest. Get it all out. Tell them how you feel wholeheartedly and honestly. Don't worry about anyone finding the letter because the next step is burning the letter! Once you have completed the letter, at the bottom of the paper, write, "I now release this relationship," and toss the letter into the flames and allow the fire to transmute the energy.

STEP 1 - CUT CORDS

Close your eyes, and get to a place of silence and calm. Invite Archangel Michael to come in and cut any energetic umbilical cords with his sword. Envision each cord attached to you with another end attached to someone else. Whether you want to keep the person in your life or not, no one should be depleting your energy or vice versa. Cut all cords you see, even if you don't know who they belong to. Inhale as you visualize Michael preparing his sword, and exhale as the connection is severed, each time, leaving you lighter, freer.

STEP 2 - ESTABLISH INTENTION

The pure intention of letting someone go is powerful. It is simple; no visualization or ritual necessary. Sometimes, all that is required is for a person to recognize they need to release a relationship. Bringing awareness to a situation that may have been going on far too long is powerful. Release your guilt, acknowledge that this is what YOU need, and use pure intent to let go.

POINTS TO REMEMBER:

1. Not all relationships you release will have ended unpleasantly. Sometimes we feel we are ready to move on, so do not allow guilt to hold you back. Do not fear hurting the other person, either. If you are intuitively being led to separate from someone, it is not always because they have done something to harm you, and that's okay! Honor what you feel, and trust that this is also what is best for the other party.

2. Sometimes, we are not releasing communication or a physical relationship, but are severing a dependency (the cutting cords method is best used for this instance). For example, you may have a friend you wish to keep in your life but need to be able to put yourself first and not continue to allow them to suck you dry whenever it serves them. By detaching and putting some distance between you and your friend, you can enhance your relationship.

3. The most important type of relationship release is mourning how relationships used to be. For example, if your sex life changed after having kids, maybe sex drastically changed because of painful, physical changes in your body. For too long, you may cling to what the relationship used to be and become stuck and unable to move forward. But when you let go of how things were in the past and mourn what used to be, you become free to allow something new to emerge. You may need to release the relationship in the past to make room for the future.

4. Often, past relationships we think are over may still be lingering in our spiritual body. Are you subconsciously holding on to an ex-partner? Simply make the conscious decision to release that person to remove the vibration of the relationship in your energy field.

PALO SANTO

Have you heard of Palo Santo?

Palo Santo is a sacred holy wood used by Shamans and indigenous people of the Andes. Don't worry, no trees are hurt in the process of selling these sticks. Palo Santo is always harvested from fallen limbs that have aged for 4-10 years. The smoke is used for smudging away negative energy and entities. The clearing, cleansing, and purifying powers of this wood are apparent to anyone who has ever smelt Palo Santo.

The aroma is incredibly earthy but has an indescribably amazing aromatic smell. When smelling it, you may feel relief, as if the smoke has washed all of the stress and tension from your body.

I recommend finding a spiritual shop near you to buy some, but if it is not possible, you can buy it off of Amazon! Grab a piece and start spreading the smoke all around your house and yourself! Relax, release, and enjoy!

TAKE IT EASY

You can't always be productive. Sometimes, the best thing you can do for yourself is to do a whole lot of NOTHING. You heard me. You have permission to sit on your butt for the entire day and allow the sun's vitamin D to heal you. There are so many self-help "to do's" that it can flat out overwhelm us. It can make us feel as if we are never done with the "work," so we fill our "downtime" with meditation, yoga, or things we think we "should" be doing.

Cut yourself a break, why don't you? Rest your cape, sis. You are not superhuman.

Sometimes, we can't do it all. Acknowledge that you are doing the best you can and be okay with stopping everything. And here is the most important part: don't do this with any guilt or shame attached to it! After spending the day doing nothing, don't tell your friends, "I am so lazy." That is not honoring the conscious choice you made to TAKE IT EASY! When we don't honor our decisions, we strip them of their value. There is value in doing diddly squat, but only if you recognize it as a way to recharge your batteries; not if you shame yourself into thinking you did something wrong.

BE WILLING TO MAKE MISTAKES

Chase progress, not perfection. For most women, the thing that causes the most stress in life is constantly striving for perfection. This is an impossible task, and one that will leave you feeling inadequate, anxious, and shameful, all of which are useless emotions.

Quit comparing yourself to others, and quit working towards pleasing every single person who surrounds you.

You are going to make mistakes, and you will continue making mistakes until you draw your last breath.

QUIET TIME

Shut off all electronics, put the do not disturb sign on the door, and even turn off the music.

It is very important to have silent, alone time. It is in the silence we can find our breath. In the silence, we make space for healing life force to move through us. Sit in stillness just watching the ocean and waves crashing onto the shore.

Find serenity in the silence. If you have children, make it a routine for the whole family to have "quiet time". For kids, instruct them to their room and advise them not to come out until you get them. They are allowed to do whatever they want in the room, like play with dolls or read a book, as long as it's quiet. Aim for an hour every day.

JOURNAL

The benefits of establishing a journal practice are endless. Journaling promotes creativity, helps to develop our intuition, helps us set our intentions, and allows us to let go. I like to finish off my morning meditation practice with a short journal session. Take the opportunity to allow whatever is inside you to spill out onto the page. Putting pen to paper allows emotions you were not even aware you had to surface. Through ink and a beautifully bound journal, you can tackle your biggest issues and can confront your ego. Journaling allows you to get out of your head and into your heart. In fact, our hands are a direct link to our heart, so writing is very much an intuitive, clairsentient experience. There is no right or wrong when it comes to journaling, but in case you need help getting started, here are my three favorite practices:

1.   Gratitude: When we give thanks, we provide a direct link for joy. Through gratitude, we manifest continued happiness. Take the time to write down 5 things you are grateful for in your life, 5 things you are grateful for about yourself, 5 things you are grateful for in your career, 5 things you are grateful for in your finances, and 5 things you are grateful for in your health.

2.   Affirmations: The statement "I am" attracts the energy of what you want to you. If you want, wish, or desire things in life, do not ask for them in the future tense. Assume you already have them and affirm "I am". For example, if you hope to one day own your own
business, affirm, "I am my own boss." Write down at least 10 affirmations you wish to embody.

3.   Letter to God: This is my absolute favorite. It is like talking to a friend. You get to vent, express all your troubles, then ask for help. For Divine intervention in your life, you need to grant your angels and God permission to do so. Release your cares to them, and they will help.

GROUNDING

As humans, we are constantly struggling with our first three chakras. Our first three chakras are all about grounding, standing in our power, stability, self-acceptance, self-love, and balance! Balance is key to living a content life, and we cannot find balance without learning how to ground down. A tree cannot grow tall without strong roots.

By establishing your own stable roots, you can open up to your intuition and easily tune into your soul Self. When you're grounded, you can step into alignment with your true Self more easily. Without anchoring your energy, you can feel anxious, detached, flighty, and uneasy about where to settle. When you are properly grounded, the earth takes your negative energy and transmutes it into positive energy.

HOW TO GROUND

STEP 1 - Go outside and plant your bare feet in the earth. Your body absorbs free electrons from the earth, and then sends whatever negative energy is consuming you back into the ground to be recycled.

STEP 2 - Hug a tree! Trees are alive, and the art of hugging them isn't just for hippies. While you are hugging the tree, maybe even listen to see if he/she has a message for you? Trees are the kings of grounding!

STEP 3 - Close your eyes and imagine a bright ball of white light above your head. Visualize this white light traveling down your head, through your neck, trickling down your arms and
fingertips, filling your chest, stomach, and pelvis, journeying down your legs, and finally, flowing out of your feet and into the ground. As you are doing this, imagine all areas of tension and possible spots where negative energy has pooled, flowing out of your body with the white light, like a waterfall, cleansing you. Then, visualize the earth's energy coming up through your feet and filling up every part of your body, leaving you feeling stable and secure.

STEP 4 - Anchor yourself like a boat. This takes literally one second and is my favorite thing to do when I am on a plane. Imagine you are dropping an anchor from your tailbone and see it fall heavily into the center of the earth. Feel yourself securely tied to the earth like a kite on a string.

HAND MUDRAS

Mudras, yoga in your hands, are an ancient art used by the Chinese, Buddhist, and Hindus. Yogis stimulate these energy locks in the hands to seal in energy and desired effects. There is literally a mudra for everything from digestion to Divine consciousness. Some favorite mudras are: Kali Mudra, Hridaya Mudra, the Tse Mudra.

It is believed that depression is caused by a lack of the water element, and Tse Mudra revitalizes this missing energy. Use Tse Mudra for comfort and support. You can add the Tse Mudra to your five-minute meditation practice in the morning or sit for a few minutes, eyes closed, consciously and intentionally breathing. Practice this Mudra whenever you need to feel more secure or are burdened with depression.

1. Sit comfortably with your legs crossed.
2. Place your hands on your knees, palms up.
3. Touch the base of your pinky finger with your thumb.
4. Cover your thumb with your four fingers.

ESSENTIAL OILS

The healthy human body vibrates at a frequency of 68 MHz. Canned food is measured at 0 MHz, fresh produce is at 10MHz, fresh herbs are 20MHz, and finally pure essential oils take the lead with up to 320MHz!

Emotions such as grief and depression, illness in the body, or an imbalance in our chakras, can bring the body as low as 40 MHz. Essential oils, the essence of plants, have the power to raise your body's frequency!

These little magic bottles strengthen and ground your energy field, release heavy, repressed emotions, clear your chakras, and brighten your aura. It is important to be picky when purchasing essential oils because only pure, certified therapeutic grade oils have the potency to create a powerful, deep, and lasting effect. Many of the oils available in the grocery store are diluted (even if they say 100%!). Make sure oils are FOOD GRADE, which are safe for internal and external use.

HEART CHAKRA

Our greatest power in life comes from our heart, as our heart is the seat of our soul. From our heart, we learn to give and receive love, we express our creativity, we FEEL through life, and we discover our joy. People often use the expression, "My heart is so full, it could literally burst!" They are feeling the unbridled intensity of the Heart Chakra.

Tune into your Heart Chakra, and you will find that your world will burst wide open. Feel your way through life, trust your heart, love fully and wildly, allow others into your heart, and receive and give EQUALLY. Power your life from your heart, and you will always be happy. Live from love, and EVERYTHING will fall into place. Use your Heart Chakra to lead you, guide you, protect you, and rejuvenate you.

Tools to support the Heart Charka include:
- Crystals - Emerald, Tourmaline, Jade and Rose Quartz
- Archangel - Raphael
- Color - Green
- Element - Air
- Yoga Poses: Wheel, Camel, Cobra, and Dancer
- Essential Oil: Basil

SOCIAL MEDIA DETOX

I go out of my way to ignore negative media and filter my exposure to strictly positive content. Some people may call this naive or ignorant. However, I don't need to surround myself with negativity to know that it exists in the world. We are all brutally aware of the heartache in our world, so why remind yourself of this every day? There are negative forces at work in our Universe, there is no denying it, but when you feed into the drama, feed into the destruction or the horror, you are giving power to this negative force.

I choose to surround myself with beauty. The vibrations you infuse your aura and soul with effect your energy body, and ultimately, your health and well-being. When we were young, our parents censored our movies, music, and even our friend groups. At times, we thought this was absurd and unnecessary, but there is validity to their reasoning. Through the Law of Attraction, you will ultimately match the same frequency of the people, things, and places you encircle yourself with. For example, when we watch horror movies, nightmares take root in our psyche. Here are suggestions to monitor your exposure.

1. Set filters on social media, and unfollow people who generate drama or negative news constantly.
2. Fill the house with beautiful things that make you smile! Flowers are my favorite option, pictures of loved ones, and gorgeous quartz crystals.
3. Do not watch disturbing movies! Comedy, anyone?
4. Surround yourself with people that lift you up. Let go of social settings that are heavy or low vibrating.

HUMAN TOUCH

Humans need touch, but it is something many are, unfortunately, deprived of having regularly. Whether it is a shoulder to lean on, a hand to hold, a friend to embrace, or a lover to touch, human interaction is a fundamental part of life. As Michelangelo said, "To touch is to give life". Touching is the way we express love to one another, and giving and receiving love as we already know is key to taking care of our soul. A single touch can release oxytocin, "the love hormone", and alter your emotional state instantly.

If you feel overwhelmed or stressed, ask for a hug.

With an embrace, you'll feel supported. Whether it be the touch of a lover, a mother, or a friend. A simple hug lets us know we are not alone, and we have another human to walk this earth with.

The Science of Touch research from Dacher Keltner has found that "people can not only identify love, gratitude, and compassion from touches but can differentiate between those kinds of touch, something people haven't done as well in studies of facial and vocal communication."

So, next time you feel exhausted, overwhelmed, or depleted, find someone, ANYONE, and ask for a hug. And, left arm over and right arm under puts the left side of your chest together, hugging heart to heart.